The FA Cup
Fifty Years On

The FA Cup
Fifty Years On

Mark Metcalf

SPORTS BOOKS

Published by SportsBooks Ltd

Copyright: Mark Metcalf 2010

SportsBooks Limited
PO Box 422
Cheltenham
GL50 2YN
United Kingdom
Tel: 01242 256755
Fax: 01242 254694
e-mail   randall@sportsbooks.ltd.uk
Website www.sportsbooks.ltd.uk

All rights reserved. No part of this publication may be produced or transmitted in any form or by any means, including photocopying and recording, without written permission of the publishers. Such written permission must also be obtained before any part of the publication is stored in any retrieval system of any nature.

Cover designed by Alan Hunns

Typeset in Palatino LT Std

A CIP catalogue record for this book is available from the British Library.

ISBN 1899807 91 8

Printed in the UK by CPI Bookmarque, Croydon, CR0 4TD

To the Blackburn Rovers and Wolverhampton Wanderers players and fans who shared their memories.

Contents

Prologue 1

The Beginning 3

Getting Started 26

The Third Round 29

The Giant Killers 50

The Fourth Round 65

The Fifth Round 76

The Quarter-finals 88

The Semi-finals 105

Leading up to the Final 116

The Week before Wembley 125

The Final 141

Appendix One
The FA Cup results round by round   159

Appendix Two
Blackburn and Wolves teams   171

Appendix Three
Other Blackburn and Wolves finals   175

Postscript   211

Prologue

NOWADAYS THE FA Cup is dominated by the big four clubs – Arsenal, Chelsea, Liverpool and Manchester United. In the last 21 years only Tottenham, Everton and Portsmouth have disturbed this hegemony.

And since Manchester United, the most successful FA Cup team with eleven victories, were persuaded not to defend the trophy in 1999–2000 in order to play in the Club World Championship in Brazil, the world's oldest competition has taken a battering.

The influx of overseas managers into the Premier League has led to some clubs preferring to rest players in favour of the league, further diminishing the appeal of the Cup.

Fans growing up with the Premier League as their yardstick could be forgiven for thinking the FA Cup is almost an irrelevance. Yet fifty years ago the FA Cup was the most important competition in the football world, with more than half the teams in the League owing their record attendances to the competition.

In 1960 no club would have contemplated scratching from the tournament as United did, while followers of Newcastle United, Bolton Wanderers, Manchester City or West Bromwich Albion (who between them won the FA Cup on six occasions in the 1950s) would never have accepted seeing their clubs roll out a reserve side for an FA Cup tie. It was normal to see crowds double, rather than halve, in size.

Players and fans alike dreamed of Wembley in May. Winning the First Division title might have been more highly regarded, but the FA Cup final, followed by millions in Britain and across the world on TV, was the cherry on the cake.

The Beginning...

The 1959–60 competition once again captured the imagination of fans across the country, excited by the giant-killing exploits of non-league Bath City and Peterborough. There was also Fourth Division Watford's thrilling run, not to mention some great games which included a sensational six-goal East Lancashire derby between Burnley and Blackburn, the outcome of which still riles older fans of the Clarets.

Ultimately it was Wolverhampton Wanderers and Blackburn Rovers who were to make it through to the final. At the time Wolves were a powerhouse of the First Division, failing by just one point to become the first team in the twentieth century to do the double of League and Cup. And while Blackburn were sitting in much the same league position as they do now, two of their team, captain Ronnie Clayton and play-maker Bryan Douglas, were back at Wembley four days after the final to play for England against Yugoslavia.

Fifty Years On

This book quotes extensively from the Blackburn and Wolves players so we introduce them now:

Blackburn

Goalkeeper – Harry Leyland. After a frustrating time as Jimmy O'Neill's deputy at Everton, the 26-year-old was given a free transfer from his home town club in the summer of 1956. He was due to move to Southern League Tonbridge, only for Blackburn's then manager, Johnny Carey, who had been in charge at Goodison Park, to step in before he played a competitive game for the Kent club. When Jack Patterson was injured the new man did well enough to make the number one spot his own.

Short and chunky, he was deceptively agile. Leyland was at his best when faced with a one-on-one with an opponent, with a textbook technique of going down bravely at an opponent's feet. Leyland's best performance in the 1960 FA Cup was in the semi-final against Sheffield Wednesday where he did much to ensure that Rovers won a tight game 2-1. Off the field he was an active PFA representative who later became the association's chairman. Leyland was to make 188 first team appearances for Blackburn, moving in March 1961 to become player-manager at non-league Wigan Athletic.

Right-back – John 'Tank' Bray – a totally committed strong-tackling right-back for whom no cause was ever lost. This made him a firm favourite with the fans and his teammates. Bray made his debut in the 1959–60 season and played in all Rovers' FA Cup games. In a career blighted by persistent leg injuries Bray made 185 appearances for Rovers before moving to Bury in April 1965.

Left-back – Dave Whelan. Now better known as the man who on retirement built JJB Sports and is chairman of Wigan Athletic. Whelan was a hard-working, tough-tackling and bustling full back, born in Yorkshire but brought up in Wigan. He had to bide his time before switching from his more natural right to left-back to replace Rovers legend Bill Eckersley. Whelan was ever-present in the Rovers FA Cup side as they made their way to Wembley in 1960, where he was to become another victim of what was known as the 'Wembley injury hoodoo' at a time when there were no substitutes. He made 78 first team appearances before moving to Crewe Alexandra.

Right-half – Ronnie Clayton made his first team debut for Rovers at just sixteen and was at his peak in 1960 when he replaced Billy Wright as captain of the England team. Rated by many as the complete old-fashioned wing half, Clayton was a tireless competitor, a good passer of the ball, and noted for his heading abilities. Towards the end of his Rovers career, in which he made 665 appearances, he showed his class by fitting easily into the back four during a period when new formations such as 4-2-4 were being developed.

Centre-half – Matt Woods helped form the dynamic halfback line with Clayton and Mick McGrath that took Rovers out of Division Two in 1958. Also signed by Johnny Carey from Everton in 1956, for £6,000, he was an inspirational figure who would have been in the reckoning for international honours had it not been for the permanent presence of Billy Wright at number 5 in the England set-up. Woods made 307 appearances for Blackburn. He went on to turn out for Luton and Stockport County and also played in Australia.

Left-half – Mick McGrath signed aged 18 from Home Farm in Dublin in August 1954. A player of great positional acumen, he was a deceptively strong tackler with a hardness that belied his stature. He helped Rovers to win promotion to the First Division in 1958 and made 312 first team appearances by the time he left to play for Bradford Park Avenue in March 1966. He also played 22 times for the Republic of Ireland. It was McGrath who grabbed two vital last-gasp equalising goals in the matches against Blackpool and Burnley to keep Rovers in the FA Cup in 1960.

Right-wing – Louis Bimpson was signed by Rovers in November 1959 from Liverpool where as deputy to the great Billy Liddell between 1953 and 1959 he had scored 39 goals in 102 first team appearances.

The Beginning...

A powerful, committed, honest centre-forward, he found himself pushed to the right wing as Bryan Douglas had to move from there to replace Roy Vernon, who had joined Everton, at inside forward. Bimpson's most memorable match during the 1960 FA Cup run was at White Hart Lane, where he scored two of his total of eight goals for Rovers. He made just 29 appearances for Rovers before moving to Bournemouth in February 1961.

Inside-right – Peter Dobing, born in Manchester, was just 17 when he made his debut in September 1956 for Rovers. An inside forward who could also play centre-forward, his career record of 104 goals in 205 first team appearances for Rovers shows his keen eye for goal and during the 1958–59 season he scored 24 league goals. Pacy, aggressive and a superb taker of free kicks, Dobing was transferred to Manchester City in 1961 before having a successful ten-year career at Stoke City.

Centre-forward – Derek Dougan was one of the game's most colourful characters. Fast, aggressive, argumentative and an awkward opponent, Dougan moved to Blackburn from Portsmouth as the new boys attempted to cement their position in Division One following promotion in 1958. It was Dougan's brace that helped Rovers overcome Sheffield Wednesday in a tight semi-final but an injury meant no one could be sure he would play at Wembley until the very last moment. And he shocked his fellow players and fans by asking for a transfer on the eve of the final. He eventually left Rovers in the summer of 1961, having scored 34 goals in 76 appearances. He went on to represent Aston Villa, Peterborough United, Leicester City and Wolverhampton Wanderers, as well as his country, Northern Ireland, before retiring. For eight years from 1970 he was chairman of the PFA. He later became chief executive and chairman at Molineux.

Inside-left – Bryan Douglas, the son of a Blackburn train driver, scored 11 times in 36 appearances for England. A brilliant passer of the ball, Douglas had the vision and clarity of thought that created opportunities for those around him. He could also trick and tantalise defenders and had a body swerve that would send opponents darting in the opposite direction. Although he played mostly on the right wing, he scored 100 goals in 438 appearances for his only club. He played magnificently on his return from injury at Tottenham Hotspur in the fifth round of the 1960 FA Cup, before moving to inside-left to supply quick through balls to attackers. Although he stood only 5ft 5ins tall, Douglas was a giant as a footballer and played for England at the 1958 and 1962 World Cup finals.

Left-wing – Ally MacLeod was born in Glasgow into a fanatical footballing family. Two of his uncles were professionals and his father was an amateur goalkeeper despite losing a leg. As a youngster he quickly showed enough ability to turn professional.

The Beginning...

As an outside-left he started at Third Lanark, joining St Mirren after National Service. He was another of Johnny Carey's signings in 1956 and he scored 17 times during the promotion season of 1957–58.

Hugely popular with the Ewood Park faithful, he earned the nickname 'Noddy' as result of the unusual bobbing motion of his head when running. MacLeod was quick, could cross a ball and he could score goals, grabbing 47 in 193 Blackburn games. He was Scotland's manager when they went to Argentina for the 1978 World Cup. He died in 2004 after suffering from Alzheimer's disease for a number of years.

Manager – Douglas 'Dally' Duncan did not have the stature as a manager of his Wolves counterpart, the legendary Stan Cullis, but he had played more times for his country, Scotland, than Cullis had for England and he had one precious possession that Cullis did not – an FA Cup winner's medal.

Duncan, who spent his entire career in England, played fourteen times for Scotland, scoring seven times, and this was in an era when the Scots often failed to pick 'Anglos'. The Blackburn manager started at Hull City, where he was nicknamed Dally for his nonchalance on the touchline, but at 23 he joined Derby County, where he played nearly 300 games despite the Second World War cutting into his career. The other winger at Derby was England international Sammy Crooks and they made an impressive double act.

While at Hull, Duncan had made it through to the 1930 FA Cup semi-final against Arsenal and when he scored to make it 2-0 it looked like the Tigers were going to Wembley. But the Londoners forced a replay, which they won 1-0. Three seasons later Duncan again suffered semi-final disappointment when Manchester City beat a Derby County side he signed for in March 1932 by three goals to two.

However, in 1946, aged 37, Duncan, collected his winner's medal as Derby County, driven by two stellar talents in Raich Carter and Peter Doherty, beat Charlton Athletic 4-1. Bert Turner turned Duncan's shot into his own goal for the opening goal of the game.

The closest Duncan came to a championship medal had been ten years earlier in 1935–36 when Derby finished runners-up to Sunderland. Duncan ended his Derby career when he moved to Luton Town as player-coach in October 1946. His most notable game for the Hatters was in a thrilling 4-3 victory over Newcastle. When George Martin retired as manager Duncan took over in June 1947, hanging up his boots at the same time. After taking Luton to third in the Second Division in the 1952–53 season, Duncan went one better in 1954–55, moving the club into the top flight of English football for the first time.

Although they went on to finish in the top half of the first division for the next three seasons, ending eighth in 1957–58, opinion on Duncan appears mixed. In *The Luton Town Story* written by Timothy Collins, he writes: "Many of the players felt his reputation

The Beginning...

exceeded his ability as a coach or motivator, but equally, just as many confessed it was Duncan's sheer technical excellence as a player and commonsense as a man which won him his success...."

When Johnny Carey left to take charge at Everton, Duncan was appointed by Blackburn Rovers, taking over a team newly promoted to the First Division. After finishing in a respectable tenth position, Duncan's side enjoyed a good start to 1959–60 and were lying second on Christmas Day 1959. However, a terrible record in the second half of the season, in which only eight points were gained from nineteen matches, saw Rovers finish just three points clear of relegation.

His Blackburn players also had mixed feelings about their manager's ability. Bryan Douglas says that the manager went on so long about his success at Luton that some players wondered what club they were at. He fell out with Rovers' inside-left Roy Vernon and could not command the respect he was shown at Luton for the achievements he made as a player.

Following the FA Cup final defeat Duncan was asked to resign, but, having signed a contract, he refused, which allowed him to claim compensation when he was sacked and replaced by Rochdale manager Jack Marshall in July 1960.

On leaving Ewood Park Duncan retired from football and moved to Brighton to run a guesthouse. He had another claim to football fame, however. His daughter Elsie married Don Revie, the former

England and Leeds United manager, who won the FA Cup as a player with Manchester City in 1956 and as a manager with Leeds in 1972.

Dally Duncan died in 1990.

Wolverhampton Wanderers

Goalkeeper – Scotsman Malcolm Finlayson was signed from Third Division South side Millwall, for whom he made 230 first team appearances, in the summer of 1956 as cover for regular England keeper Bert 'The Cat' Williams. Although he made only 13 first team appearances in his first season, Finlayson became the regular Wolves keeper in 1957–58, when Wolves were the only First Division side to concede fewer than 50 league goals during the season, a record maintained the following season as they won back-to-back league titles.

Finlayson was an agile performer with a safe pair of hands, was courageous and commanded his area with distinction. He played in five of the seven Wolves FA Cup games in 1959–60, by which time he had already started out in the business world. He later became, and remains successful as, a director of R&F Stockholders of Kingswinford near Dudley. Finlayson would undoubtedly have won caps for Scotland had their selectors not decided on a policy of no 'Anglos'.

The Beginning...

Right-back – George Showell from Bilston was signed by Wolves aged 15 in 1949, but it was not until April 1955 that he made his debut at right-back in a 1-1 draw with Preston North End. Showell enjoyed an eight-match run to the end of the season as replacement for Eddie Stuart. But Stuart's form over the following four seasons restricted Showell's appearances in the first team. Showell, however, performed with honour at centre-half when Billy Wright was on England duty, but failed to make the place his own when the Wolves legend retired at the end of the 1958–59 season. He captured the right-back spot after Stuart was given a hard time by sections of the Wolves crowd during a home match against Luton Town on February 23rd 1960 and kept it on the run-in to Wembley. He made 218 appearances.

Left-back – Gerry 'The Horse' Harris signed for Wolves after an unsuccessful trial for West Bromwich Albion, He took over as left-back from Bill Shorthouse in 1956. A tireless competitor, Harris had a keen positional sense and could pass the ball as well as tackle. He played more than 270 first team games for Wolves before moving to Walsall.

Right-half – Eddie 'Chopper' Clamp made his debut as a 20-year-old at Old Trafford but it wasn't until the start of the 1957–58 season, when Wolves won their second league title in five seasons, that he made the right-half spot his own. His form was good enough to earn him a call-up for England and he was a member of the 1958 World Cup Squad in Sweden, where he played three games alongside his Wolves halfback colleagues Billy Wright and Bill Slater. Nicknamed 'Chopper', Clamp was a resolute performer, a no-nonsense player with a crunching tackle. After 241 appearances he left Wolves for Arsenal in November 1961 before moving to Stoke City the following year

Centre-half – Bill Slater, born in Clitheroe, was part of the Blackpool team beaten by Newcastle United in the 1951 FA Cup final. After a year at Brentford, Slater joined Wolves at the start of the 1952–53 season, becoming the first team right-half the following season as Wolves took the league title. He won two more championship medals in 1958 and 1959 during a period when he appeared for England at the 1958 World Cup. Switched to play centre half during the 1959–60 season, he performed so superbly that only days before the FA Cup final he was voted Footballer of the Year. He played 333 games for Wolves, scoring 25 goals. Captain of the side at Wembley in 1960, Slater was awarded an OBE and then a CBE.

He was Deputy Director of the Crystal Palace Sports Centre. He became Director of Physical Education at Liverpool and then Birmingham University. He was Director of National Services from 1984 until 1989, when he was elected as President of the British Gymnasts association. His daughter Barbara became the BBC's first female head of sport in 2009.

The Beginning...

Left-half – Ron Flowers was one of the all-time Wolves greats, who by the time he moved to Northampton Town in 1967 had made 512 first team appearances and gained three League Championship medals and an FA Cup winner's medal. Flowers developed a superb partnership with inside-left Peter Broadbent, which helped make the Wolves side of the 1950s into one of the finest ever seen in England. Between 1955 and 1966 he played 49 times for England, including the 1962 World Cup finals in Chile. He was a member of England's 1966 World Cup winning squad but did not play a match. In 2009, along with the other non-playing members of the squad, he received a belated World Cup winner's medal – a fitting tribute to a fantastic footballer.

Right-wing – Norman Deeley stood just 5ft 4ins tall but once he broke into the Wolves first team at the start of the 1957–58 season he became a giant on the pitch. Eight months later he collected the first of two league winner's medals and scored 23 league goals. Quick, always full of running and able to beat an opponent, Deeley also had a healthy goals total of 75 from 237 games by the time he moved to Leyton Orient in February 1962. Deeley made two appearances for England and played in all seven of Wolves' 1960 FA Cup ties.

Inside-right – Barry Stobart was a product of Wath Wanderers, Wolves' Yorkshire-based nursery club. Unable to dislodge Peter Broadbent or Jimmy Murray, it was not until five years after he signed professional forms that he made his first team debut at centre-forward on March 5th 1960. The Cup final was only his sixth first team appearance and his second at inside-right but he was chosen instead of Bobby Mason. By the time he left to join Manchester City in the summer of 1964 he had made only 54 first team appearances.

Centre-forward – Jimmy Murray was a prolific goalscorer, averaging more than one every two games. Able to hit the ball with both feet, he was quick and, in a side accustomed to using the long ball, always available. Murray had the knack of being in the right place at the right time. He was the top scorer in both of Wolves' successful league title seasons at the end of the 1950s as well as in 1959–60 and later in 1961–62. Murray played in six of Wolves' seven 1960 FA Cup ties, missing only the quarter-final at Filbert Street against Leicester City.

Inside-left – Peter Broadbent was Wolves' playmaker for much of the 1950s. Broadbent won three League Championship medals and one FA Cup winner's medal in either inside forward position, hammering home an impressive 145 goals in 497 first team appearances. A superb passer of the ball, he was an elegant, beautifully balanced player, unfortunate to make only seven appearances for England, one of which was at the World Cup finals in Sweden in 1958. Competition in the shape of Bobby Charlton,

The Beginning...

Johnny Haynes and Bobby Robson restricted his opportunities. He was revered by Wolves fans of the day, one of whom – Steve Gordos – has written an excellent biography.

Left-wing – Des Horne was born in South Africa in December 1939 but moved to England and signed for Wolves in December 1956. In 1958 he was a member of the successful 1958 FA Youth Cup winning side and the following season he scored three first team goals in eight matches. Horne started the 1959–60 season in the reserves but made the outside-left position his own after performing superbly at Luton Town in early October. Although he did not play in the semi-final, and looked at one point to be missing out on a Wembley appearance due to the fine form of Gerry Mannion, a defeat at home to Spurs saw him return for the final league match at Chelsea, where he was brilliant.

Lightning quick and with an eye for goal, Horne was never regarded as the brightest of players and was instructed by manager Stan Cullis before the final to run with the ball towards the large R on the Radio Times billboard behind one goal before crossing the ball into the box for the likes of Jimmy Murray and Norman Deeley! Horne was transferred to Blackpool in March 1961 after 52 games and 18 goals.

Manager – Stan Cullis was a manager who must surely rank alongside men such as Sir Matt Busby, Sir Alex Ferguson, Bill Nicholson, Bob Paisley and Bill

Shankly. Cullis built two great Wolves sides; the first won the 1949 FA Cup and the League five years later. As players came towards the end of their careers he slowly replaced them – Bill Shorthouse retired, Bert Williams was replaced by Malcolm Finlayson, Norman Deeley came in for Harry Hooper, who had been bought to replace Johnny Hancocks, and Jimmy Murray for Roy Swinbourne, and from 1956 to 1961 Wolves had a second great team.

Cullis had moved up from assistant to replace Ted Vizard, sacked in the summer of 1948. The measure of his success can be gauged from the nine-year period starting in 1952–53. Wolves finished outside the top three only once, in 1956–57 when they were sixth. And in those days money did not talk as it does now.

Born in Ellesmere Port, Cheshire, in 1916, Cullis wanted to move into journalism but his prowess at football was such that several clubs checked him out and he signed for Wolves. His playing career was cut short by the Second World War but between February 1934 and May 1947 he made 171 first team appearances, largely at centre-half, for Wolves and also earned 12 full international caps, along with 20 wartime caps.

A natural leader, he captained Wolves for several years, during which time he led them to the 1939 Wembley FA Cup final, a match in which Portsmouth confounded the critics by winning 4-1. Although he was a powerful tackler and strong in the air, it was his ability with the ball that marked him out. Cullis was able to split a defence with precision passing and

The Beginning...

on occasions he would also dribble his way through to create chances.

His final game as a player was against Liverpool at Molineux on Saturday May 31st 1947. Wolves would have captured the league title for the first time had they won but Liverpool were also in contention. If they beat Wolves and Stoke failed to win at Sheffield United the Merseyside club would lift the First Division trophy for a fifth time. A draw would have left Wolves in top spot awaiting the Stoke result from Bramall Lane two weeks later. Things couldn't have been tighter.

The key moment of the match came midway through the first half when a chipped ball over the Wolves' defence left Albert Stubbins in the clear. Cullis was left stranded; stopping his opponent would mean bringing him down from behind or grabbing hold of his shirt.

Today it would be a certain sending off, but not back in the 1940s when it might not have even brought a booking.

Cullis refused to consider fouling Stubbins, who duly notched the winner in Liverpool's 2-1 victory. Stoke lost at Sheffield and Liverpool were champions.

Cullis played hard but fair, his attitude summed up perfectly by his later statement about the incident: "Why I didn't bring him down or pull Stubbins back by his shirt – and I suppose I could have done. But I didn't want to go down in history as the man who decided the destiny of the championship with a professional foul."

When Cullis took control of first team affairs, Wolves had just finished fifth in the league but had gone out of the FA Cup in the fourth round to Everton after a replay. Under his direction Wolves roared to Wembley in 1949. The following season they lost out narrowly to Portsmouth on goal difference for the First Division title. Four seasons later they won it, pushing near neighbours West Bromwich Albion into second place. This first title triumph was followed by a second at the end of the 1957–58 season and a third in 1958–59.

Despite these successes, Cullis was not without his critics, who argued that they were built on a long-ball game. It was claimed that skill was sacrificed for hard work and stamina. Cullis certainly made sure that he got 100 per cent effort from all his players, and anybody who failed to give it soon found himself being moved on.

His management principles were clearly outlined when he said: "No club can hope to succeed in the tough competition of football unless the players combine in their personality three principal factors. They must have tremendous team spirit, they must be superbly fit, and they must use the correct tactics on the field." Cullis's genius was to achieve all three.

Team spirit was garnered by ensuring that everyone was treated equally. Billy Wright might have been Wolves' biggest star during the 1950s but even he could expect a tongue-lashing if he played badly. Cullis was also scrupulously fair – players

The Beginning...

who'd been at club for five years were entitled to a bonus of £750 – a serious sum of money at the time. At many clubs players who had rarely featured in the first team might find themselves being given a much reduced benefit. Not at Wolves. When winger Malcolm Clews reached five years with only one first team game under his belt there was no question of him not getting the money.

Malcolm Finlayson gives a further example of Cullis's commitment to people who gave their all for him: "In 63–64 Stan let me continue playing part-time as I was moving into business. But in September 1963 Roger Hunt trod all over my hand up at Anfield and broke it. This took me six or seven weeks to recover and then when I got back playing it was in the reserves at West Brom. I got kicked on the knee and after that I decided to call it a day as it meant I was having to get taken in the back seat of my car to work and back. Cullis, however, made sure I got paid till the end of the season. He was as straight as a die, was Stan.

"He was a hard manager, straight-talking and wouldn't suffer fools gladly but he would never criticise his players in public or in the press and I know that he really helped out one or two Wolves players who fell on hard times. I'd say his bark was worse than his bite, although not to journalists who I witnessed at times waiting to go in and interview him and were shaking like a leaf.

"In the 1980s I had my house burgled and they took my two league championship and FA cup winner's medals. Stan, and Gordon Taylor, from the PFA, unknown to me, got the FA and the Football league to replace them. It was great of them I must say."

Spirit and fitness were all well and good, and certainly not to be decried, but it was Cullis's belief in what amounted to the "correct tactics" that sometimes earned him the derision of fans and newspaper columnists and which probably still accounts for the fact that the Wolves teams of the 1950s are rarely mentioned as being amongst England's finest.

This is in spite of the fact that, apart from Huddersfield in the '20s, Arsenal in the '30s, Liverpool in the '80s and Manchester United most recently no other club has enjoyed such a period of sustained success. And none of the others scored a hundred league goals a season for four consecutive seasons as Wolves did, with a combined total of 422 between 1957 and 1961.

The reason is because of the tactics Wolves employed. They were based on Cullis's own intensive study of tactics used by rival First Division clubs. He concluded that getting the ball forward as quickly as possible relieved the pressure on the defence and increased it on opponents. Cullis was also aware that playing conditions in the English winter, which turned pitches into either mud baths or dangerously rock hard, were hardly conducive to silky ball-playing skills.

Cullis's plan was to employ two quick wingers and a fast centre-forward to run on to direct long passes

The Beginning...

played into space, from which they could take on their opposing full backs and centre-half, most teams then employing a back three. In the first period of Cullis's managerial spell at Molineux, Jimmy Mullen and Johnny Hancocks were the wingers with Jesse Pye and later Roy Swinbourne at centre-forward.

By 1960 it was Norman Deeley and Des Horne out wide with Jimmy Murray through the middle. Wolves scored 106 league goals in the 1959–60 season, with Murray getting 29 of them, three behind Manchester United's Dennis Viollet, the league's top scorer that season.

Sunderland's Stan Anderson, an England international who played against the Wolves sides of the 1950s and was part of the Roker Park team that beat them in the 1954–55 FA Cup quarter-final, sums up the feelings of many from that period when he says: "Wolves were a very strong, determined side composed of players that gave 100 per cent. They had Billy Wright, who was a very solid player who read the game very well.

"Stan Cullis adopted a style of football that was based on speed and athleticism rather than skill on the ball. It was very effective and they scored a lot of goals but I am not sure it was that attractive to watch."

Of course, with Wolves beating virtually every team put in front of them it was difficult to be overly critical – after all, Cullis was paid to win football matches and Wolves fans of that period are deservedly proud of their favourites.

And Cullis had an attention to detail that was radical; his support for his players, fitness training and team spirit building were innovations, as Helenio Herrera suggested after Barcelona routed Wolves in a European Cup quarter-final at Molineux.

Ken Jones, a football writer with the *Daily Mirror* and later a columnist with *The Independent*, was with Stan Cullis the night before he was sacked. He remembers it well: "I always got on well with Cullis. Many journalists were afraid of him. That was also the case with most or his players, who he treated badly and would openly ridicule, such as when Eddie Clamp got injured playing against Vorwaerts of East Germany in the European Cup when he got done whilst trying to hurt one of their players. As he was getting taken off his manager was laughing as much to say 'so you think you're hard'.

"On one occasion a journalist at the now long gone *Daily Herald* heard that all the players had decided to stand up for themselves by putting in transfer requests. The story came out in the paper's first edition, which at that time would be out on the London streets at about 10.00pm. Stan used to have a column in the *Sunday Express* at the time and Alan Williams used to ghost it. He rang Stan and only got to tell him what had happened after he'd been told off for ringing so late. The following morning the outside of Molineux was packed with journalists but nothing happened as none of the players turned up with their transfer requests – they simply didn't dare.

"The night before Stan Cullis got sacked was after

The Beginning...

he'd been ill and was not long back at work. He was outlining to me how he intended rebuilding the side but I hadn't even had time to complete my column the following day when I found out he'd been sacked – he clearly had no idea it was coming. Cullis was too honest to have spoken to me the way he had if he knew he was on his way out. With Stan it was a case of either 'take me as I am or leave me'."

Getting Started

THE FA CUP proper in 1960 consisted of six rounds, the semi-finals, and the final. Before the first round there were qualifying rounds to find which non-league Clubs would enter the competition alongside teams from the third and fourth tier of the Football League – known in 1960 as Division Three and Four respectively.

The magic of the competition derives from the fact it is a knockout, with the possibility of upsets. This meant in 1960, and still does, that even the smallest of clubs with no chance of winning the cup could create their own particular piece of history.

In 1933 Third Division Walsall knocked out League champions Arsenal, while in 1949 southern League side Yeovil put out First Division Sunderland. Non-league clubs could, and often did, record smaller but still notable victories over league sides. The 1960 tournament was to be no different with successes for four non-league sides.

When the 1959–60 tournament began the holders were Nottingham Forest, who had defeated Luton Town 2-1 in 1959, winning the trophy for only the second time. Wolves were intent on capturing a cup they'd last won in 1949 while Blackburn had not won the competition since 1928.

The competition began with the preliminary round

Getting Started

on September 5th 1959 when 78 teams wrestled for the right to win through to the competition's first qualifying round two weeks later.

Those taking part included three ex-league clubs in Darwen, Nelson and New Brighton. Also appearing were a club set to go on to capture the famous trophy three decades later when they beat Liverpool 1-0 in the 1988 final. Wimbledon easily beat Dorking 6-0 to join up with Cheltenham Town and 142 other sides in the first qualifying round. These teams might have no chance of winning 12 games to capture the FA Cup but they were going to give it their best shot.

The first round proper was played on Saturday November 14th, when the 30 qualifiers were joined by 48 League clubs from Divisions Three and Four as well as the previous season's FA Amateur Cup finalists Crook Town and Barnet. Forty would make it through to the second round.

Four non-league sides – South Shields (1936), Bath City, Peterborough and King's Lynn – beat league sides in Chesterfield, Millwall, Shrewsbury Town and Aldershot respectively. And amateur cup winners Crook Town made it through to the second round by beating Matlock Town 1-0 after a replay. The FA Cup had clearly lost none of its glory for surprises.

One poignant note from the first round, although they didn't know it at the time, was that Gateshead had played their final FA Cup match as a league club. They lost 4-3 at home to Halifax in a game watched by 4,570. At the end of the season they failed to win re-election to the league.

The second round saw Crook Town lose out 1-0 at home to York City, while King's Lynn lost 4-2 at Reading before a crowd of 16,991. South Shields (1936) also fell, beaten 5-1 at home to Bradford Park Avenue. Southern League Margate, however, would have beaten Crystal Palace had Arthur Roberts not spurned three great chances. The league side ensured there was no second chance in the replay, winning 3-0. But Peterborough beat Walsall 3-2 in a thrilling game watched by a ground record crowd of 20,600 at Fellows Park. Their reward was a third-round tie against Alf Ramsey's Second Divison Ipswich at Portman Road. Bath City also made it through to the third round by winning 1-0 away at Notts County.

Former England manager Graham Taylor has fond memories of those days. "All those years ago, when it was an FA Cup Saturday, I just could not wait to tune in and listen to the wireless to find out if there had been a shock result. I mean, this was the FA CUP."

The Third Round

SPURS WERE viewed by bookmakers as favourites to win the Cup with odds of 11-1, while Wolves were 12-1, Blackburn 22-1 and Luton, the previous season's losing finalists, were long shots at 66-1. The first favourites in the competition's first year of 1872 were the Royal Engineers. They were 4-7 and they lost.

There was to be a certain symmetry in that the clubs which ended up playing in the FA Cup final started their campaigns with away ties in the north-east, Wolverhampton Wanderers taking on First Division 1950s Cup giants Newcastle United and Blackburn Rovers visiting Second Division Sunderland.

Having captured the First Division trophy for the second consecutive season at the end of the 1958–59 campaign, Wolves, formed originally by the amalgamation of St Luke's Blakenhall and the Wanderers, justified their position as second favourites.

The Black Country side had won the cup on three occasions, although only one victory had come at Wembley. This was in 1949 when Wolves beat Leicester City of the Second Division 3-1.

Wolves fans' hopes that this would be the start

of a period of cup success were, however, foiled over the next few seasons, including by Newcastle United in 1951. Playing at Leeds Road, Huddersfield, Newcastle won a replayed semi-final 2-1.

The Geordies won the final with two goals by Jackie Milburn against a Blackpool side featuring a youngster who became the last ever amateur to play in the final. His name was Bill Slater, and by January 1960 he was halfway through his eighth season with Wolves.

In 1951 Slater had returned home disappointed from Wembley by train straight after the game. He was under instructions from his teacher-training college in Leeds to be back as soon as possible. Joining him in his carriage were dozens of Newcastle fans who, luckily for Slater, failed to recognise him.

He remembers: "Today I think it would be difficult for a player to combine playing with teaching. I stayed as a teacher for so long because of the element of security. With football you could always get injured or the manager might not like you and you wouldn't then get a game.

"Anyway, I really enjoyed being a teacher so I just carried on doing it after I finished my football career. It's true that after signing as an amateur for Wolves in 1952 I later succumbed to pressure to turn professional although I always had a proviso where teaching came first. So I missed one or two games. That included a European Cup match at the Nou Camp against Barcelona during the season we won the FA Cup."

The Third Round

Slater had not only swapped clubs by 1960, moving from Blackpool via Brentford to the Black Country, he'd also swapped positions, from wing to centre half.

He recalls: "We won the First Division title in the previous two seasons but Billy Wright retired at the end of the '58–59 season. We struggled to replace him – no surprise really; Billy was a marvellous player and also a marvellous man. Billy was almost irreplaceable.

"The manager, Stan Cullis, tried various players at centre-half, including George Showell, who'd played there with distinction when Billy was away on international duty. But it was quite a gap to fill. It wasn't coming right and we struggled in the first part of that season.

"I played wing-half but one day Stan Cullis said to me, 'I am going to play you centre-half.' It was a request you couldn't refuse, certainly not from the likes of Stan Cullis, but as I had never played there it was still a gamble!

"Anyway, the third time I played there was at Newcastle away in the FA Cup. At centre-half you had to be more cautious than playing at wing-half, where your responsibilities were to support in attack and get back to help out your defenders. In those days the defence was a centre-half and the two full backs and we usually had a player each to mark. The game was more attacking then. Nowadays they emphasise defence and at times you've got a single forward and three or four defenders, which as well as making the game less exciting means a defender has a much easier time."

This view is also shared by Matt Woods, the man who was to be Slater's counterpart in the Blackburn team at Wembley in 1960. "I feel that centre-halves have it easy these days. In my day you'd regularly end up with two forwards bearing down on goal with only yourself to try and stop them; sometimes it was three. Now they have two centre-halves even if there's only one centre-forward. I can't see how any centre-half can have a bad game these days."

Woods had joined Blackburn Rovers, then in Division Two, after a torrid five-year period at Everton. His description of experiences at Goodison Park provides an example of why Slater settled on the side of caution when faced with choosing between a teaching job and a career as a professional footballer in the 1950s.

"At Everton I started played in the 'B' team and I did pretty well and so they asked me to sign amateur forms as I was only 15. When I later signed professionally it was one of the worst things I ever did as I soon discovered the manager, Cliff Britton, hated me. And I hated him. In those days they could keep you even if you wanted to move. Well, I wanted to move. I was on the list for five years. When you signed for 12 months you were like bonded for life, at the end of it, and even if you wanted to move on they could just keep you.

"They said I could move but then they didn't tell me about clubs who might be interested in signing

The Third Round

me. They did tell me no one had enquired but I know that wasn't the case.

"By the end I was on top money and I was in the reserves. I only played about eight games for Everton all the time I was there. At one point I got into the first team. We played away at Sunderland, who'd been doing really well, and we drew 0-0. We then beat Villa 2-1 at home and Huddersfield 5-1 when I scored – yet the manager dropped me for the next match at Cardiff which was lost 6-1.

"I only managed to get a move when Britton resigned. They wanted to keep me but I was glad to see the back of the place and going to Rovers was just wonderful. I never regretted it for a single second," says Woods, who was desperate for a decent cup run after Rovers had fallen at the semi-final hurdle two years previously, losing somewhat unfortunately 2-1 to local rivals Bolton Wanderers at Maine Road.

That defeat and another semi-final failure in 1952 against Newcastle was the closest Blackburn Rovers had come since winning at Wembley in 1928 to adding to the club's impressive haul of six FA Cup victories. Rovers' record put them equal second with Newcastle, just one behind Aston Villa, whose victory in 1957 against Manchester United had taken them to seven.

Both centre-halves fancied their chances in the FA Cup that year.

Says Woods: "I felt confident we'd do well in the FA Cup as we had a good side and we weren't frightened of anyone. What you want is to get home draws, of course. As it happened we didn't get too many but we battled through."

Says Slater: "Although we hadn't done so well in the FA Cup the previous couple of seasons I always felt if we played as well as we could that no one would beat us."

Of course, their team having won the FA Cup three times in the previous nine years, Newcastle's fans were having none of that. Malcolm Finlayson remembers when booking into the hotel before the match that fans were telling him they'd already arranged their own transport and hotels for Wembley in May. Newcastle had also just hammered Manchester United 7-3 with Len White scoring a hat-trick.

Such confidence did not appear misplaced when in the 18th minute Ivor Allchurch opened the scoring. A free kick from Alf McMichael was pushed back into the goalmouth by Gordon Hughes and Finlayson was unable to get both hands on the ball, which left the Newcastle number 10 with a simple chance. The vast majority of the crowd of 62,350 went wild with delight. According to Manchester United manager Sir Matt Busby, Allchurch was such a good player that "he never needed a number on his back for identification. His polish, his class could not be missed. He vies with the greatest of all time, yet he has a modesty that becomes him."

Shortly after the goal, Hughes missed a chance to make it 2-0 and his side were made to pay in the 32nd

The Third Round

minute. A free kick from Ron Flowers was knocked back to him. He blasted it back and the ball touched a defender and floated away from the unsighted Brian Harvey in the Newcastle goal. The estimated 4,000 Wolves fans, who included 72 who'd chartered a flight to avoid the seven-hour train journey, were relieved. Steve Gordos, later to become sports editor at the Wolverhampton *Express and Star*, was one of those on the train with his father.

He recalls: "My dad, who was the son of a Russian Jew, could recall Wolves bringing back the cup in 1908. He went to the 1921, 1939 and 1949 finals. He was a real fanatic of the club. My dad booked a carriage on the train up to the first match at Newcastle, and he had erected on the front of the engine a sign saying 'Taking goals to Newcastle'. That was my dad: he had a great sense of humour."

Six minutes later Wolves were in the lead. A corner from Des Horne was not properly cleared and when Norman Deeley pushed the ball back towards goal, Dick Keith handled on the line leaving referee Jack Kelly no option but to award a penalty. Eddie Clamp struck this confidently past Harvey.

Newcastle tried desperately to force an equaliser before half-time and it took a last ditch tackle by Eddie Stuart to deny centre-forward Len White. White, though, was instrumental when Newcastle did pull level. Just after the break he sent a superb pass to George Luke which was pulled back across the goal for George Eastham to force home the second home goal.

Fifty Years On

With Newcastle being roared on by their fanatical supporters, Slater showed just what a good player he was in whatever position. In his *Express and Star* match report 'Commentator' wrote that "Slater was playing really brilliantly". He awarded him the Man of the Match.

Gordos recalls the atmosphere at St James' Park, saying: "I had never heard such noise in my life. You could get a roar at Molineux but nothing like I heard at St James' Park. It was absolutely deafening. It was a good result for Wolves." Especially so as they were on a poor run with only one victory in the previous five matches.

The replay was fixed for the following Wednesday evening.

Ten miles south-east at Roker Park, Blackburn Rovers also trooped off with a replay to look forward to, having drawn 1-1 with Sunderland before a crowd of 34,129.

The match was a hard-fought affair which saw both teams reduced to ten men when Blackburn inside forward Roy Vernon and Sunderland youngster Alan O'Neill were involved in a tussle 15 minutes from time and sent off by referee Arthur Holland. Blackburn had taken the lead three minutes before through Peter Dobing and seemed set to go through at the first attempt.

However, within seconds of the restart the Sunderland right-half and captain Stan Anderson broke through to pull the ball back for Ian Lawther to

The Third Round

equalise with a neat backheel flick. In 1961 Lawther would replace Derek Dougan at Blackburn.

Blackburn had only themselves to blame. They had squandered a number of first-half chances with Ally MacLeod being the main culprit. After missing a gilt-edged opportunity in the first minute he appeared to lose confidence.

MacLeod, later to achieve fame and notoriety as manager of Scotland, had arrived at Blackburn not long after completing his national service. His wife, Faye recalls: "Ally was very much a home bird and had no idea where Blackburn was, but he was more than happy to go south after Johnny Carey, who everyone knew from his time at Manchester United, travelled up specially to speak to him.

"My husband always said his stay at Blackburn was the most enjoyable in his time in football. There was a very good atmosphere at Blackburn. What I think helped was the fact that amongst the side only Bryan and Ronnie were local lads. The rest were from different parts of the United Kingdom and we socialised quite a lot – there was a very close relationship between the players and the wives.

"Sadly it ended pretty poorly. Ally felt he wasn't being properly rewarded after the maximum wage was lifted not long after the cup final. After he agreed a move to Hibs, Blackburn actually offered him more money to stay but he felt he couldn't break an agreement and we moved back north. His wages as a footballer were always more than the average man's but we didn't live a rich life.

"At the matches we'd just get seat tickets for the grandstand but no fuss was made of us and there was certainly no room set aside like there is today."

Centre-forward Derek Dougan also had a poor match at Sunderland with the reporter in the *Blackburn Times* writing that he "came off second best in his duel with the giant Hurley." Charlie Hurley, the Sunderland centre-half, played for the club from 1957 to 1969 and was later voted as the club's Player of the Century.

Ironically, Blackburn had taken the lead in the 72nd minute during Sunderland's best spell. Harry Leyland did well to keep out a number of shots from around the edge of the area. But at the other end Peter Dobing struck MacLeod's short corner between the unsighted keeper Peter Wakeham and his near post.

Woods says: "There were no easy games in the FA Cup in 1960 as it was the major cup competition in England. It was every boy's dream to play at Wembley, even those who never played professionally! The match at Sunderland was a tight, hard-fought match that I feel we should have won. Roker Park is a good ground and Sunderland had fanatical fans, still have, but by managing to get a draw I was confident we'd beat them at home."

Bryan Douglas says: "The match was a typical no-holds-barred cup tie in which Sunderland were backed by a very partisan crowd."

Confirmation of just how important the FA Cup was in those days comes from Anderson, who was to represent England on a couple of occasions and be part of the World Cup Squad in Chile in 1962.

"In 1955, when Sunderland got through to the semi-final of the FA Cup, we were also doing very well in the League. I can recall the players sitting around having a chat and Len Shackleton was going on about how it wasn't possible to win both the League and the Cup in the same season. As the FA Cup Final in those days was possibly the biggest game in the world – it was certainly watched by more people on the television than the World Cup final – he was all for taking it easy in the League in the run-up to the semi-final. That's what happened and we lost two crucial games, one of which was at home to Arsenal, who we had beaten easily away that season.

"We ended up losing our semi-final and when we lost the following weekend at Chelsea it went a long way to ensuring they went on to win the League. I still think I could have ended up winning the League that season. To make matters worse, of course, we lost in the semi-final the following season as well and I never got anywhere near a Wembley final after that," says Anderson, who at least did get to run out at the famous ground when he played for England against Austria in 1962.

A Second Division club did manage to put out one from Division One in the third round although it could not be entirely regarded as a shock. Second Division Aston Villa lived up to their FA Cup reputation by knocking out Leeds 2-1 at Elland Road. It was not a surprise. Leeds had an abysmal cup record. The last time they had won an FA Cup tie was in February 1952 when they beat Bradford Park Avenue. They finally ended the run in 1963 when they beat Stoke City 3-1.

But there was a massive shock for the 42,605 packed into Maine Road, where Manchester City, sitting uncomfortably close to the First Division relegation zone, were beaten 5-1 by Southampton, who would go on to be Division Three champions that season. Winger Terry Paine was the outstanding player on the field and according to Richard Dewar in the *Sunday People* he "tore the City defence to shreds and laid on four of the goals." Dewar gave Paine 10 out of 10 in his rankings.

After beating Newport County 4-0 at Somerton Park, First Divison leaders Spurs were still the bookies' favourites. There were reports that Wolves were interested in signing the Third Division team's talented young centre-half Ollie Burton to plug the gap left by Billy Wright but he could do little against Tottenham as Bobby Smith, the man he was supposed to be marking, put the Londoners ahead after six minutes.

The goalless draw between Stoke City and Preston North End at the long gone Victoria Ground was a dull affair enlivened only by what went on off the pitch. Referee Arthur Ellis, who had officiated at the 1952 FA Cup final and the first European Cup final four years later, was offered a bribe.

This came to light after the replay when Don Hardisty wrote in the *Daily Mail* that "Ellis was last night trying to trace the two men who offered him a £25 bribe to 'fix' the FA Cup tie. Before Saturday's game at Stoke he received a letter offering him £25 if he would swing the game in PNE's favour. The letter was followed by a mysterious phone call offering the same bribe. Mr Ellis reported the matter to the FA."

The Replays

There were six thousand fewer spectators for the second meeting between Blackburn and Sunderland than at Roker Park. All but 250 were home fans, and they saw a game in which the result was never in doubt.

It was clear long before the final whistle that Blackburn would be playing near neighbours Blackpool in the fourth round. Even when Sunderland did get themselves back into the match with a goal from Alan O'Neill on 57 minutes the Second Division team conceded a third within a couple of minutes to give themselves far too much to do.

The game was played on a damp, floodlit pitch with the away side – initially at least – pushing forward and there was a hectic scramble in the home goalmouth at the end of which Leyland was left injured and in need of treatment. Douglas then forced the first real save of the match, Wakeham stopping the England international's powerful drive.

With Blackburn continuing to press, Sunderland were forced back, but with few real opportunities the match seemed likely to be goalless at half-time only for Vernon to collect a header by Louis Bimpson, sidestep Hurley and give Wakeham no chance. Len Ashurst then appeared to have kept Sunderland's hopes alive by scrambling a Bimpson effort round the post before, with seconds of the first period left, Wakeham gifted Blackburn a second by allowing MacLeod's half-hit shot to slip through his hands and legs and trickle into the net.

Sunderland's reply came after Irish international Ambrose Fogarty's pass into the middle was lifted over Leyland by Lawther. The shot hit the bar but O'Neill was on hand to push it over the line. The tiny band of away supporters who'd made the difficult trip from the north-east at last had something to cheer but two minutes later Vernon split the defence with a magnificent pass which allowed Bimpson to run clear and restore the home side's two-goal advantage.

With six minutes remaining Vernon completed a wonderful performance with a powerful shot that Wakeham could not stop although he got two hands to the ball. Len Ashurst hit the bar shortly afterwards – it would have been his first Sunderland goal – but Rovers ran off worthy winners.

Mick McGrath was a big fan of Roy Vernon, saying: "On his day he was virtually unplayable. Roy had this sense of confidence that meant he always wanted the ball, which could make things difficult when he played with Peter Dobing, as Peter also always wanted the ball. They'd argue about who should have it although not at free kicks as Roy was brilliant as a dead-ball free-kick specialist and certainly was as good as, say, David Beckham."

McGrath also considers himself fortunate to have played in the same side as Ronnie Clayton. "Ronnie Clayton was a marvellous player. No man who played so many Rovers and England games could fail to be. He was a great captain, too. He didn't go round bawling at players but he would be quietly urging you to do your best and if you made a mistake he'd tell you to forget it and just concentrate on your game. Off the field he was very good company. To play your best you need a good atmosphere at a club and Ronnie was vital in making sure we had that at Blackburn.

"Ronnie and I were the half backs for many years in the Rovers side. I was the more defensive one of the partnership and my job was to get the ball and give it to Ronnie and Doug (Douglas) and let them play. Ronnie had a very good partnership with Bryan. Ronnie had good balance and if you passed him the ball he'd control it quickly and pass it on if he was under pressure. He also could get forward quickly and he could hit balls, which don't forget in those days weren't the lightweight ones of today, from right-half over to the left winger with ease. Not many players could do that at the time."

Bryan Douglas remembers "feeling very confident we'd go through against Sunderland. It took a bit of time to break down the Sunderland rearguard, in which Charlie Hurley was the outstanding player and didn't give Derek Dougan much of a chance of scoring. But when we eventually scored I didn't think Sunderland had the forwards to break down our defence. By the end we were well in control of the match."

Len Ashurst remembers: "The Blackburn side contained two very good players in Ronnie Clayton and Bryan Douglas. Ronnie was a very talented wing half with good vision, a quality passer and although he was a big lad he didn't indulge in any rough stuff. He was one of a number of really good wing halves at the time. Bryan always gave me a difficult time when I played against him. He was quick and tricky on the ball and it was natural that with his skill he would play many times for England."

Wolves also scored four times in their replay and while Newcastle got one more than their north-east neighbours the home team earned themselves a home fourth-round tie with Second Division Charlton Athletic.

This was always going to be a special occasion. The famous floodlights at Molineux were going to illuminate an FA Cup tie for the first time and it promised to be another of those wonderful Wolverhampton football evenings.

The Third Round

It had been only four years previously that the FA had finally relented and allowed competitive matches to be played under lights. Wolves had pioneered floodlit football, playing friendlies against Honved and Spartak Moscow in 1954 and Moscow Dynamo a year later. It helped promote the club on the world stage.

Going into the game Wolves knew that history was against them as no team had beaten Newcastle in an FA Cup replay for twenty-four years.

Molineux was an intimidating ground to visit. The most imposing feature in 1960 was the enormous South Bank, which accommodated some 30,000 spectators.

Perhaps the bitter cold and snow kept the crowd down to 39,082 but they watched a thrilling match. Newcastle took the lead on nine minutes when Finlayson was given no chance as White powerfully headed home a cross from Gordon Hughes. The Tyneside team were, however, unable to enjoy this success. Within a minute Wolves were level when 19-year-old George Heslop, deputising for the injured Bob Stokoe, took an impetuous swing at the ball. It spun off his foot to make it easy for Jimmy Murray to guide it inside a post.

Just six minutes later Bryan Harvey was forced to pick the ball out of his net for the second time when Norman Deeley fastened on to a fine pass from Peter Broadbent to beat him with a powerful drive.

The game swung back Newcastle's way and George Eastham took advantage of hesitancy by

Fifty Years On

Eddie Clamp to bring the scores level at 2-2. Again Wolves struck back immediately. Ron Flowers hammered a fearsome shot from more than 30 yards that hit a post before going in to give Wolves a 3-2 lead.

Flowers had been signed from Wath Wanderers, based at Wath-on-Dearne near Barnsley. Set up and run by Mark Crook, a former Wolves teammate of Stan Cullis, it was the country's first ever 'nursery club'. A lively winger, Crook had bought a Yorkshire fish shop on retirement and in his spare time set out to train youngsters. Wath was just ten miles away from Flowers's Doncaster home and, frustrated at the lack of action at Belle Vue after he signed as an amateur, he was only too glad to join Wath.

By the time he moved to Wolves in the summer of 1951 another Wath Wanderers product, Roy Swinbourne, was already established in the Wolves first team at centre-forward. The inevitable "Grapes of Wath" headline appeared when Flowers broke through to the first team.

Many more sportsmen went through the Wath system. Indeed, Wolves' opponents Newcastle United were one of those to have benefited most from Crook's undoubted talents. They snapped up two players who'd moved into professional football at Barnsley from Wath. Jorge Robledo and his younger brother Eduardo were born in Chile to an English mother and Chilean father. Because of political instability in Chile they emigrated in 1932, when Jorge was five and 'Ted' four. When in January 1949 Newcastle approached Barnsley asking to sign Jorge he

The Third Round

refused to move unless Ted came with him. The Tyneside club duly signed both players.

Two years later George wore the number 10 in the 1951 FA Cup Final, against Bill Slater for Blackpool, and the following year he was joined by his brother at number six as he rammed home the only goal that saw the Geordies retain the trophy by beating Arsenal 1-0. Not surprisingly they remain the only brothers from outside the United Kingdom to have played in the same side in an FA Cup final.

The Robledos had gone by 1960, as did any hopes of a Newcastle recovery at Molineux. In the 50th minute Des Horne intercepted a pass from Alf McMichael. The Northern Ireland full back was one of the most experienced players on the pitch but he naively rolled a ball through the snow to Heslop and Horne nipped in to make it 4-2.

In his report in the *Express and Star* the following day, 'Commentator' gave special praise for the half backs Eddie Clamp and Ron Flowers and remarked that "Bill Slater had come through yet another game with the hallmark of class in everything he did."

It appeared that Wolves had at last found someone to take the place of Billy Wright, giving them a great chance of winning the FA Cup and perhaps even the 'Double' of Cup and League glory last achieved by Aston Villa in 1897.

Malcolm Finlayson remembers: "The match was one of those where the pitch was cleared of snow and blue lines painted on it. It was bitterly cold and would probably have been postponed today. Bill had a good game.

"A goalkeeper is the only player who can see everything that's happening on the field. He can tell for example if a player is trying to go down the blind side of a defender and make him aware of the danger. You have to make sure you command your area and you have to be constantly talking to those in front of you and they have to be aware that if you're coming for the ball then it's yours.

"Bill listened if I said anything. He could also play and had good ball control, helped no doubt by the fact that he had previously been an inside forward."

One pundit was already predicting a Wolves run on Wembley. In the *Daily Mail* John Ross wrote "Beware! These Wolves have a Wembley look."

There were other replays that evening. The biggest surprise came at Upton Park, where Huddersfield Town, from the Second Division, thrashed Division One West Ham United 5-1.

The victory was put down to two factors. One was that the Yorkshire team decided on rubber boots, which helped them stay upright on the slippery surface. The other was that Denis Law was in the form that was to make him one of the world's most feared attackers. Law did not score but he was involved in all five goals.

A couple of months later the Scottish striker was signed by Manchester City for a British record fee of £55,000 and he went on to further glory with Torino.

The Third Round

Meanwhile, after their goalless draw at Gigg Lane, Bolton Wanderers and Bury were meeting at Burnden Park. And Third Division Bury showed that Saturday's draw had been no fluke by going out of the FA Cup only after extra time against their more illustrious rivals. Bury were only 15 minutes away from recording their first victory in four ties against their near neighbours. They were 2-1 ahead until Bolton equalised through Ray Parry. Bury's record crowd of 43,616 saw Parry wrap up the tie by scoring in the 118th minute to make it 4-2.

There can surely be no greater indication of just how important the FA Cup was to fans fifty years ago than the three ties played between First Division Arsenal and Second Division Rotherham United. They drew 2-2 at Millmoor and 1-1 at Highbury before the lower league side triumphed 2-0 at Hillsborough.

The Highbury replay attracted their biggest crowd of the season – 57,598. And although the Gunners totally dominated the game they were forced to settle for a third chance the following week. Even at a neutral venue this second replay attracted an attendance of 56,290!

They saw Rotherham record a famous victory with goals from Keith Kettleborough and Brian Sawyer. The Arsenal manager, George Swindin was gracious: "It was completely one-sided. Rotherham thoroughly deserved their victory. We never hit our game at all."

The Giant Killers

Bath City and Peterborough United

GIANT-KILLING HAS a special place in FA Cup history; the thought that a team from the lower divisions can upset one of the elite appeals to the English psyche and every great club has at one time or another been conquered by the unfancied, unheralded and sometimes unknown.

Since its inception the tournament has had the reputation of being a 'great leveller' by inspiring lowly clubs to play above themselves while bringing the bigger clubs down to their opponents' level. Perhaps the biggest FA Cup giant-killing act remains Walsall's 1933 Fellows Park defeat of First Division giants Arsenal, then in their pomp in the middle of a spell in which they won the League four times in five years and finished runners-up the other year. After the war Yeovil of the Southern League beat Sunderland in 1949. The 1950s also saw some major cup upsets with Boston United winning 6-1 at Derby County in 1955, Newcastle United falling at home 3-1 to Third Division Scunthorpe United in 1958 and in 1959 Manchester United being put out of the competition 3-0 by Third Division Norwich City.

The Giant Killers

York City of the Third Division North also made it all the way to the semi-finals in 1955, beating Blackpool and Spurs from the top flight before finally falling to Newcastle United, but only after a replayed semi-final. There had also been a shock for the mighty Wolves, beaten in January 1957 by lowly Bournemouth 1-0 at Molineux.

The seemingly impossible does happen – especially in the FA Cup. It remains the essence of the tournament and in 1960 it was no different with two non-League teams, Bath City and Peterborough United, capturing the imagination of millions of football fans across England and further afield. They wouldn't make the final but they would leave their mark.

Tony Book, the Manchester City captain from the 1969 FA Cup final and for four years in the 1970s their manager, was an important member of the Bath City team at the time.

He remembers: "A lot of the players, including myself, worked for the chairman's large building firm, and on cup tie weeks we were allowed to go down and train during the day rather than do a day's work and then train in the evening. That was a big bonus.

"We used to get decent crowds of around three to four thousand but at the cup matches they would more than double and you'd get an extra thrill playing in front of a larger crowd. It was a great period in my life: we also won the Southern League that year and we scored a lot of goals as well.

"We had Charlie Fleming up front. He was the best goalscorer I had ever played with at that time and the best striker of the ball I have ever seen, and that includes some of the great players I later played with and against. He used to stroll through games and one time I mentioned this to the manager and he said 'Tony, he gets you the bonus most weeks,' which was correct."

Fleming was a Scottish international signed in July 1958 from Sunderland, where in 1955 and 1956 he was an FA Cup semi-final loser. He scored 48 goals in all matches as Bath successfully chased the Southern League championship in 1959–60 and in all grabbed 216 goals in seven years.

Bath City had started that season in fine form and were top of the Southern League when they travelled the short distance to play local rivals Yeovil Town in the fourth qualifying round.

Their 2-0 victory was followed by news they'd drawn Fourth Division Millwall at home in the first round. Confidence was high that the London side would be added to a list of conquered League clubs that included Crystal Palace, Southend United and Exeter City.

Having hung a lucky horseshoe surrounded by Scottish heather in the dressing room before the Yeovil match there was no way that Bath were not going to maintain the tradition. Long before kick-off a large queue of eager spectators had already formed.

The team wore new shirts for the special occasion and even though every Bath spectator was hoping to see their side win there was still a cheer of welcome from them when the first Millwall fans, sporting blue and white rosettes, arrived in the ground two hours before the match got under way.

The 10,000 packed into Twerton Park witnessed a thrilling performance by the Southern League side, who overcame Millwall in a match described by KGG in the Monday edition of the *Bath and Wilts Chronicle and Herald* as "being a rough and tough one. It was certainly no teddy bears' picnic... with a player on either side sent off. O'Neil of Bath and Wilson of Millwall were involved, and early in the second half, they were ordered to the dressing rooms". The duo were reported later to have continued their scuffle, along with another Millwall player not involved in the match.

Bath took the lead on 25 minutes through centre-forward Peter Wilshire. This came after club captain Fleming and Book opened up the Millwall defence. Having done the hard work by getting in front, the home side then relaxed and paid the penalty when within a minute Millwall were level after Joe Wilson equalised.

However, when Fleming lashed home a free kick just before half-time home fans' hopes again soared and they were not to be disappointed when, with 11 minutes left, Frank Meadows scored with a delightful chip. "When the final whistle sounded hundreds of fans invaded the pitch to praise the team for a wonderful performance," said KGG.

Their reward was another Fourth Division side,

Notts County, at Meadow Lane. There was a best-of-season crowd of 25,869, including some 4,000 West Country fans, making it the largest attendance ever to watch Bath City. Having won nine consecutive matches at home, County, the oldest club in the Football League and winners of the FA Cup in 1894, were expecting to progress but on the day the Bath goalkeeper Ian Black was, according to KGG, outstanding and "has probably never played a better game in his life".

Having battled to half-time without conceding a goal, Bath took the lead three minutes into the second half when Joe O'Neil finished off a fine move by the wingers Dave Wring and Peter Thomas.

Bath were now in the draw for the third round, joining sides from Division One and Two. The draw was attractive even if it was not one of the super clubs. They were at home against Second Division Brighton and Hove Albion. With a big crowd anticipated, the club decided to erect a temporary stand and this helped in creating a record crowd of 18,026.

The current treasurer of the supporters' club, Graham Weeks, was one of them and he remembers it as a very special day.

"I got down to the ground at 11.30am to make sure I was at the front. As it happened the local paper used a photograph they'd taken of me which I have still got. I'd never seen such a big crowd before. As a youngster it seemed absolutely massive, but I never felt frightened or anything as everyone was just so excited.

The Giant Killers

"Bath hadn't reached the third round of the FA Cup for many years but what added to the excitement was the fact that there were TV cameras at the match, which in those days was still a bit of a novelty, making it a very special occasion for any spectators and those who played in the game. A truly great day."

Not surprisingly, manager Bob Hewison selected the team which had disposed of Notts County and Bath entered the match with their confidence high, having won 19 out of their last 20 games, the only defeat coming at Headington United (later renamed Oxford United) in November.

Despite this fine record, however, the Brighton manager Billy Lane had confidently predicted that his side would "win at the first attempt". Afterwards he was to admit that "we could not have grumbled if we had lost."

The single goal that settled it came with 20 minutes to go after the Bath left-back Ian MacFarlane failed to clear and Brighton right winger Mike Tiddy, with the breeze behind him, drove the ball from 30 yards against the inside of the post and into the net. The defeat was to be one of only nine in 53 games that Bath played during a season in which they scored 150 goals with only 58 against. Ian Black, the keeper signed that season after a career with Aberdeen, Southampton and Fulham, which included one international appearance for Scotland, played in every match.

Brighton were pitched against Rotherham in the fourth round, going through after two replays.

Giant-killing was nothing new to Peterborough. They had made it through to the first round proper on ten occasions and in 1957 had reached the fourth round.

In 1959 they took Second Division Fulham back to London Road after a goalless draw at Craven Cottage. They lost somewhat unfortunately in the replay by a single goal and fans still wonder what might have happened had Roy Banham's shot not crashed back off the crossbar.

The London Road club were also mounting a vigorous campaign to gain entry to the Football League, hoping to replace one of the bottom four sides in Division Four – who were in those days forced to apply for re-election at the end of each season. This was not easy, however, as only one club, New Brighton, had lost their place in the League since the end of the Second World War, Workington Town replacing the Wirral club at the end of the 1950–51 season.

As the Midland League champions, Peterborough entered the FA Cup at the fourth qualifying stage, where they were drawn to play the Suffolk side Bury Town from the Eastern Counties League, running out 7-1 winners.

When Shrewsbury were picked to play at London Road in the first round it gave Peterborough a chance to add to a list of conquered league clubs which already included Torquay United, Aldershot, Ipswich, Bradford Park Avenue and Lincoln City. It turned out to be a seven-goal thriller.

The Peterborough manager Jimmy Hagan had been a fine player himself. Born in the north-east, he followed his father, a Newcastle professional, into football, playing for Derby County before signing for Sheffield United for £2,295 and making his debut in November 1938.

Following the end of the Second World War, Hagan resumed his career at Sheffield on a part-time basis, having got a job as a trainee chartered surveyor. In 1948 he won his only England cap in a 0-0 draw in Copenhagen against Denmark. By the time he retired he had scored 117 league goals in 361 league matches for the Blades after which he accepted the post of manager at Peterborough.

This was the start of a fine second career that saw him take Peterborough into the league and to Fourth Division glory in 1960–61 before he left to manage West Bromwich Albion, whom he led to League Cup success in 1966.

However, his greatest success came with Benfica in Portugal, where he won three successive championships between 1970 and 1973.

Despite his accomplisments with Peterborough, Hagan was not universally popular with the players, with one or two of them feeling his training methods lacked inspiration.

"All we seemed to do was run round the track," says Scottish winger Peter McNamee, who had joined the club although he had no real idea of Peterborough's location. "I was on National Service when the offer came in and I had to ask one or two of the lads where Peterborough was. The nearest we could get was when someone said it was the last stop before London." The Scotsman was amazed when he turned up to discover that gates of over 10,000 were a regular feature at London Road.

The tie with Shrewsbury would rank with the very best, and it was rounded off with a last-minute winner to enthuse the vast majority of the 16,300 crowd. Heavy rain turned the pitch into a quagmire although that did not deter the League side. After 49 minutes they were two up, the second scored by player-manager Arthur Rowley, who was the highest scorer in League history – 434 goals in 619 games – when he hung up his boots.

By 71 minutes the scores were level thanks to Dennis Emery and Ray Smith. Shrewsbury introduced another twist when Malcolm Starkey scored his second seven minutes later, only for Emery to make it 3-3.

"Dennis was a wonderful player," says McNamee. "He wouldn't beat people, he'd drift into space. He was a very good finisher with his heading and his scoring. We had a good partnership. He was a great character and great friend of mine and we enjoyed a drink or two together. He was, however, one of those people that never had any real luck.

"Mind you, he was daft after he was badly injured in a car crash. I urged him to tell the insurers he wouldn't be able to play again as he would have got a benefit match and I am sure there would have been a good crowd. Typical of him, he wouldn't do it. He got the insurance, which was only enough to replace the car, and he never did fully recover. He ended up going to Bedford Town.

"He died when he was young. He was also unlucky that Hagan was the manager as Arsenal wanted to sign him but Hagan wouldn't let him leave. Imagine that today, a lower league player being refused the chance to go to Arsenal!"

With the score locked at 3-3 the match was in the last minute when centre-forward Jim Rayner squeezed the ball past Shrewsbury goalkeeper Alan Humphreys. What a finish and what a match!

The reward for Peterborough – if that is how it could be described – was a visit to Walsall. It was another thrilling game, with Peterborough recovering from the shock of going behind to a Tony Richards goal after little more than 30 seconds to exploit a 15th-minute injury to Peter Billingham, which left the Walsall centre-half a passenger for the rest of the game. By 69 minutes Peterborough were 3-1 ahead thanks to two goals from McNamee and another from Smith.

"Peter McNamee was an excellent player: he was all left foot, but could beat defenders and was a fine passer of the ball," recalls Ron Cooper, who played against Bury Town and acted as 12th man during the rest of 1960 FA Cup run.

Billingham, limping in attack, showed remarkable courage to stick out a foot to deflect a cross from John Davies past Tom Daley, collapsing to the ground as the ball entered the net. But Walsall were unable to to force an equaliser and non-League Peterborough were now in with the big boys.

Having disposed of clubs from the Fourth and Third Divisions, Peterborough were given the opportunity of knocking out one from the Second when they were drawn to play at Portman Road against Ipswich Town. Their manager was former Tottenham and England right-back Alf Ramsey, the man who was to guide England to World Cup glory in 1966. He had taken over the reins at the then Third Division South side in August 1955.

Ramsey had a score to settle with Peterborough, for in his first FA Cup match as a manager Peterborough put out Ipswich 3-1 in the first round in a match played at London Road.

Ramsey was quietly fashioning a formidable team at Ipswich and they went on to shock the football world by winning the First Division title in 1961-62. But that was in the future. On January 9th 1960 Peterborough showed that their previous victory at Portman Road had been no fluke by just edging a five-goal thriller.

The feat was even more remarkable given that Peterborough were forced to play with only ten fit men from just after half-time when an injury to full back Jimmy Walker forced him to limp for the rest of the match up front, and especially as for the third time they were forced to come from a goal down to achieve victory.

Peterborough started the match on the attack with Jim Rayner forcing a fine save from Roy Bailey.

However, in the 18th minute they found themselves a goal down when Tom Daley, under pressure from Ray Crawford, later to be capped by England, failed to cut out a cross from Jimmy Leadbetter which left Doug Millward with the simple task of knocking the ball into the empty net.

Daley had been dragged out of his bed that morning after other players found him fast asleep in his Felixstowe hotel with six empty pint mugs under his bed. "It didn't seem to do him any harm, as he had a really good game," laughs Peter McNamee.

Crawford should have made it 2-0 but after dribbling past the goalkeeper the centre-forward somehow managed to miss an open goal.

Ipswich were made to pay for Crawford's failure when on 42 minutes Rayner swept confidently home. However, when Walker was badly injured just after Ted Phillips put Ipswich back into the lead in the first minute of the second half it seemed that, for this season at least, Peterborough's FA Cup successes were over. With Walker in attack, Roy Banham was pushed to full back with Rayner dropping to wing-half.

Banham was one of the few full-time professionals at Peterborough. He had signed from First Division Nottingham Forest after they'd refused to pay him an extra £1 a week to take his wages to £10. Peterborough obliged by giving him £11 a week with £2 for a win and a £1 for a draw.

Despite the changes, Peterborough equalised in the 53rd minute when Emery curled the ball past

Bailey, better known now as the father of goalkeeper Gary Bailey, who was to collect FA Cup winner's medals in 1983 and 1985 with Manchester United.

With the play swinging from end to end the only surprise was that it took until the 86th minute before the fifth goal arrived. It came when the Ipswich centre-half Andy Nelson failed to clear a corner and the grateful Emery unwrapped the gift. Many of the Peterborough supporters swarmed on to the pitch at the end to hoist the victorious players on to their shoulders and carry them to the dressing room.

Alf Ramsey was gracious in defeat, saying "All praise to Peterborough – they were the better side."

Now Peterborough faced a team from Division One in the fourth round, and it was a formidable task. Their opponents were Sheffield Wednesday, lying fourth, and the game was at their Hillsborough ground.

More than 20,000 Peterborough fans made the trip, pushing the crowd above 50,000. The visiting fans hoped to roar their side to another famous victory with their favourite song:

On to the field they run
Our team called Posh
Eleven men in blue and white
Never saw a better sight
And as the ball goes in
We'll shout hurrah
Forward, forward to a win

Shoot for goal,
Shoot for goal
POSH
(thanks to historian Peter Lane)

Those who made the trip were to be rewarded with a fine performance from their favourites, who as usual were led on to the pitch by 'Mr Posh', or Kevin McAlpine to give him his proper name. Although the teams were separated by more than 90 league places, the Peterborough players fancied their chances.

Roy Banham says: "We had a winning team and no matter what league you're in that breeds confidence. Wednesday were a good side but we'd beaten Ipswich, who were doing well in the Second Division, and although we were beaten 4-2 by Gainsborough United in between the two FA Cup matches that was because we were saving ourselves for the cup. I thought we'd get a draw."

It was not to be: the magnificent run came to an end when, with less than ten minutes remaining, Wednesday stole the lead through Bobby Craig, who added a second before Peterborough could regroup. Wednesday were slightly flattered by 2-0.

Jimmy Hagan said afterwards: "The boys were magnificent. With only ten minutes to go I thought we had earned a replay. Those snap goals were a tremendous disappointment, but Peterborough's players gave all they had... and a bit more."

Eric Taylor, the general manager of Sheffield Wednesday, said: "Peterborough have won a lot of friends by their grand performance. Everyone who saw the game had his money's worth."

Peterborough's efforts helped them win the *Sunday Pictorial* Giant-killers Cup and at the end of the season the club were elected to the league after Gateshead failed to gather sufficient votes.

The Fourth Round

HAVING BEEN beaten 11-1 by Aston Villa in Division Two in November, Charlton Athletic arrived at Molineux at the end of January with few people giving them much chance of an upset. But Scottish goalkeeper Willie Duff, so chastened at Villa Park, raised his game magnificently, making three tremendous saves in the first ten minutes. It inspired the Londoners to take a shock lead after 22 minutes when Johnny Summers dashed down the middle to shoot home.

They hung on until two minutes from half-time, when Des Horne snapped up a pass from Deeley to give Duff no chance.

Duff continued to make save after save and it seemed likely there would be a replay at The Valley, when Peter Broadbent headed in a cross from Norman Deeley. Wolves ought to have given the scoreline the stamp their dominance deserved but after Peter Broadbent was hauled down by Gordon Jago two minutes from time Duff saved Eddie Clamp's penalty kick.

Norman Dixon, writing in Monday's *Daily Express*, reported: "Duff's colleagues patted him on the back. The Wolves players clapped him. Even the rain-lashed fans stayed to give him a final cheer, as children stay to watch the magician leave the stage.

Perhaps they thought he might still wave a magic wand and put Charlton through into the next round. But no, Willie had used up all his magic in holding these worrying Wolves for so long."

Despite the penalty miss Clamp remained high in Steve Gordos's affections. He says: "I liked Eddie as a player; he was a hard man but he had a lot of football in him and he was useful both as an attacker and as a defender. I often felt that he was a lot better player than most people gave him credit for."

Bill Slater offers one of the reasons why supporters might have not given Clamp the acclaim Gordos thinks he deserved, saying: "Eddie Clamp could be a bit wild. He was not always disciplined and he always worried you; he could either be brilliant or daft. And you were never sure which one it would be."

Blackburn were also at home, in a Lancashire derby against Blackpool which pulled a crowd of 51,223 into Ewood Park. The teams had clashed in the traditional Christmas fixtures when Dougan's goal was enough to give Blackburn both points on Christmas Day, while Ray Charnley's strike reversed the scoreline at Bloomfield Road 24 hours later.

Rovers went into the match on the back of two disappointing defeats. First they were beaten 3-0 at Sheffield Wednesday, then they lost 1-0 at home to Wolves.

The Blackpool cup match generated so much interest among supporters of both sides that it was made all-ticket. Blackburn and Blackpool had met

The Fourth Round

only once in the Cup, in 1925 when a single goal from Syd Puddefoot took Rovers to the semi-final at Meadow Lane, where they lost 1-0 to Cardiff City.

Twenty-four hours of continuous rain meant a pitch inspection but it was declared fit. Blackpool included two players – goalkeeper George Farm and outside left Bill Perry – who'd played in the victory against Bolton at Wembley in 1953. Farm had made ten appearances for Scotland between 1953 and 1959 and as manager was to take Dunfermline Athletic to Scottish Cup success in 1968.

Perry, born in South Africa, although he played three times for England in 1955–56, has gone down in Blackpool folklore as the man who scored the winning goal in 1953 and thus gave Stanley Matthews his FA Cup winner's medal.

The day was dull and drab with only Blackpool's tangerine-coloured strip brightening the gloom. At the start a mist made it difficult for spectators to identify the players. Nevertheless, the atmosphere was electric.

It was the away side that started more brightly, and it was no great shock when they took the lead on 17 minutes through Arthur Kaye. With Barrie Martin keeping Bryan Douglas quiet on the Rovers right, Harry Leyland had to be at his best and the home side were grateful to go in at half-time only the single goal down.

Jimmy Mudie should have put the game beyond doubt but he miscued Kaye's free kick, allowing a grateful Matt Woods to hack clear. Perry then shot across the goal when well placed before Woods again came to the rescue, blocking a shot from Ray Charnley. Rovers were hanging on.

Dave Whelan also kept Blackburn in the game. When Charnley headed a free kick from Perry past Leyland, the left full back was expertly positioned to head off the line.

With four minutes left came the game's dramatic high point. Farm spilled Bray's high looping cross to Dougan, standing just a couple of yards from the line, and when he poked it back towards the goal a huge roar of relief went up from the home support. Farm, however, was determined to atone for his error and he hurled himself to block the ball. Some say he scooped it back from behind the line but it started a scrum that would have done justice to any match at Twickenham.

Attackers threw themselves towards the ball, desperate to kick or force it over the line; defenders refused to surrender and threw themselves at it too. These days the referee would surely have blown for a free kick or a penalty; almost certainly bookings and possibly a sending-off or two or three might follow. Newspapers would report how football was becoming ever more violent.

The referee for some strange reason had positioned himself on the right-hand post, obscuring part of the goal, and he seemed transfixed by events of which he was supposed to be in control.

Mick McGrath, a player not noted for his

goalscoring exploits, had refused to join the fray and along with Roy Vernon and Ally MacLeod held back, waiting for the ball to emerge. When it did the Ireland international steadied himself, saw the gap between Peter Hauser on the line and the referee and slammed the ball home. Blackburn had got out of jail and such was the elation among the Blackburn players that the Irish international was mobbed by his grateful colleagues – and these were the days when a goal was usually greeted by a handshake or pat on the back.

Matt Woods recalls the game: "We were fortunate against Blackpool at home. But they made the mistake of dropping a bit too deep to defend their lead and late in the game virtually every player was in their box and there was mud everywhere and the ball fell to Mick McGrath and he scrambled it in."

The scorer has this to say: "Matt is right. In the first game we were totally outplayed but they made the mistake of defending too deeply and towards the end we just kept driving the ball into the area and they'd whack it clear.

"There must have been ten players in the six-yard box; I was just outside it and when the ball came to me I just whacked it with my left foot, my weaker foot. I can remember the referee was standing just outside the upright and he was enjoying himself, smiling away. I'm glad the ball went into the net, especially as I didn't score all that many goals."

Ewood Park was not the only ground that weekend where muddy conditions made playing football tricky. Today most pitches are like billiard tables compared with some of the mud baths of the early 1960s. Often by November pitches had little grass on them and it meant teams had to try to play down the flanks, especially if it was rainy. Which is partly why most teams played with two wingers. The Blackburn v Blackpool tie was not the only that contained high drama. Bristol Rovers shared six goals with Blackpool's nearest neighbours Preston North End, then a First Division powerhouse. And Tottenham Hotspur had to travel to Gresty Road to play Crewe, emerging with a 2-2 draw.

Eastville was packed with a record crowd of 38,472, which saw the home side take the lead three times, with Alfie Biggs grabbing two. But each time Preston retaliated with Tom Finney getting their second. The third equaliser arrived when Sammy Taylor finished off a move inspired by Finney.

Fourth Division Crewe also had a record crowd, with 20,000 shoehorned into Gresty Road to watch the Cup favourites. Spurs took the lead through Les Allen after just eight minutes but Merfyn Jones equalised. Another Welshman named Jones, this time Cliff, put the First Division giants ahead. But two minutes later there was pandemonium as another Welshman, Bert Llewellyn, made it 2-2. Crewe might even have nicked the match as Bill Brown saved low down as the referee looked to blow the final whistle. Crewe were to pay for their impudence.

The Fourth Round

There was plenty of excitement in the fourth round. Aston Villa, surging towards the Second Division title, won 2-1 at First Division Chelsea in front of 66,671; Sheffield United knocked out the holders Nottingham Forest at Bramall Lane, where Derek Pace scored all three goals and the 1959 finalists Luton Town lived to fight another day by beating Huddersfield at Leeds Road. Left-winger Tony Gregory lashed home the ball with only seconds of the 90 minutes remaining and Huddersfield goalkeeper Ray Wood said, "Visibility was terrible. I couldn't see over the halfway line and in normal conditions I must have saved Gregory's shot."

Manchester United, the team Wood played for in the 1957 final when he was clattered by Peter McParland, inflicted a 3-1 defeat on Liverpool at Anfield, not surprising in that recently appointed manager Bill Shankly had not had time to put his stamp on a club languishing in the lower reaches of Division Two. The match was a personal triumph for Bobby Charlton, who in previous weeks had appeared to lack confidence but his two fine goals set up a comfortable win for Matt Busby's side.

Bill Shankly was to go on to manage Liverpool to two FA Cup final victories, the first in 1965 against Leeds by 2-1 after extra time and the second nine years later when Newcastle were destroyed 3-0 in a match that marked the end of Shankly's 15 years in charge at Anfield.

Fifty Years On

The replays

Having played so well at Ewood Park, and having lost just one of their last 20 home games in the FA Cup – a shock third-round defeat to Third Division North York City in 1955 – Blackpool were confident that Blackburn's late equaliser would be only a minor irritant.

But it was Blackburn who were in top form and Stanley Whittaker of the *Blackburn Times* reported that the away side's "slick, methodical football bore the stamp of class. Speed and poise at inside forward was their main armament."

As a result of his sending-off at Sunderland Roy Vernon was suspended, forcing manager Dally Duncan to change an attacking line-up that had been heavily criticised in the local papers after the display on the Saturday. Most offered the opinion that only MacLeod had played anywhere near his best.

Douglas was moved from outside right to take Vernon's place at inside left with Louis Bimpson coming in at right wing, a switch that was to become the norm later in the season.

Rovers were two ahead by the interval. First, after 17 minutes, Dobing scored with a low drive from the edge of the area after MacLeod and Douglas had confused the home defence. Then, just before the interval, a long throw from Harry Leyland was controlled by Douglas, who floated over a centre for the unmarked Derek Dougan to head home.

The Fourth Round

With eight minutes remaining, Dobing, who earlier in the day had completed his two years of National Service, put the matter beyond doubt by making it 3-0. Stanley Whittaker wrote: "Apart from the glorious skill of Dobing and Douglas, Rovers' strength lay at half-back where Clayton, Woods and McGrath made a formidable trio."

Mick McGrath believes it was "the best we played in the cup run. They had had some great players such as Peter Hauser, Dave Durie and Jimmy Armfield. At Blackpool Bryan Douglas and Dobing linked up so well that everything we tried largely came off. It was one of those games when things you've practised for hours on the training ground come off – it doesn't happen that often, but we were doing one-twos and little triangles with the ball. It's what you work so hard for. One of my favourite games of all time, that one was."

"We murdered Blackpool in the replay," says Woods. "We totally took them apart, but we did have some good players and when it all clicked we were capable of beating any side. I was a good footballer. I feel that my strengths as a player were my heading ability and I was a good tackler. I was not the quickest but I feel I made up for this by being able to read the game well so I could anticipate where a ball might get played and react accordingly.

"I became a professional footballer after my uncle wrote to Everton when I was just out of school. Like a lot of lads I loved playing football; to be honest, there was little else to do at the time – there certainly wasn't a television to sit in front of like today. With my mates, dozens of them, we played on the fields at Skelmersdale after school and in the holidays. The ball was different than today but it was all we knew so no one complained.

"I was playing in the Wigan Sunday League, which was an open-age league. I was 14 or 15 and played for Upholland West End – it was because of a friend of mine who I worked with at the local shoe factory. He came out of the Navy and played at Skelmersdale United. He was helping me through my apprenticeship at the shoe factory and asked me to play. I enjoyed it and was playing at wing half at the time."

Spurs were to record their record score in the replay with Crewe. Their 13-2 victory beat their 10-4 win over Everton the previous season in manager Bill Nicholson's first match. The game attracted a crowd of 64,635, including 2,000 away fans. Crewe were 10-1 down at half-time with Spurs relaxing visibly after the interval. Their scorers were Allen with five, Bobby Smith with four, Cliff Jones with a hat-trick which included a penalty and a single goal from Tommy Harmer. Crewe replied through Nev Coleman and Bert Llewellyn.

After the game, Crewe's keeper Brian Williamson said, "I never saw so many shots. It was like having ten forwards against me and a ball for every forward."

Captain Roy Warhurst said, "It was the best show of football I have ever seen."

The Fifth Round

There was praise, however, for the defeated side from Desmond Hackett in the *Daily Express*. He wrote: "I have seldom seen men so beaten still gritting their teeth and driving tired muddied legs to more effort."

Many football followers felt that Spurs had shown themselves to be poor sportsmen by continuing to search for goals after going in at half-time so far in front. Typical of them was one George Garrett of Marden Avenue, Hayes, whose letter appeared in the *Daily Express* later in the week. He wrote: "Why didn't Spurs ease up after scoring half a dozen goals? Their show-off performance is enough to shatter the morale of a struggling minor side. I hope Blackburn cut them down to size."

By a quirk of fate, the train which took the Crewe party home left platform 13 at London Euston and arrived at platform 2 at Crewe.

Tottenham's next opponents would be Blackburn Rovers at White Hart Lane.

Bristol Rovers also went down heavily in their replay, although given what happened at White Hart Lane the chances are they would have taken 5-1. If they thought that a fourth-minute penalty miss might affect Tom Finney they were disappointed. Playing at centre-forward, the former England international was sublime, and after laying on the first goal for Joe Walton in the 18th minute he scored a fantastic goal in the 55th minute when, after a dazzling 40-yard run, he slotted home.

The Fifth Round

SPURS MUST have used up all their FA Cup fortune against Crewe for they were no match for Blackburn. Spurs were missing their influential left half Dave Mackay but Rovers were without Roy Vernon, and not through suspension this time.

Former Blackburn manager Johnny Carey, now in charge of Everton, persuaded his old club to sell the Welsh play-maker for £20,000 plus Eddie Thomas, a journeyman inside forward.

In Dave Whelan's autobiography, *Playing to Win*, published in 2009, he reports that Vernon and manager Duncan clashed from the outset, Vernon walking out when Duncan first addressed the players following his appointment in 1958.

Thomas, who had made his debut the previous weekend in a 2-1 home victory against Manchester City, was available for cup duty having not played for Everton in previous rounds, but was not chosen for the White Hart Lane match. He was a good player but not in Vernon's class and Rovers fans and players were left bitterly disappointed by the loss of the Welshman, who went on to play a vital role for Everton when they captured the league title in 1963. He was top scorer that season with 24 goals.

Duncan decided to keep Bryan Douglas at inside left although he had to watch his fitness. Before the

The Fifth Round

game Dally Duncan told reporters: "Douglas cannot go full out for 90 minutes. He will have to have short rests on the right wing." He was still recovering from a cartilage operation earlier in the season and he switched between inside left and the right wing throughout the 90 minutes. Nevertheless, he was the game's outstanding player.

Spurred on by their support, stuck high up in the main stand among a crowd of 54,745, Rovers took the game to Spurs, who were three points clear at the top of Division One. Neat passing surprised the home side, who earlier in the season had beaten Rovers 2-1 in the league at White Hart Lane.

Douglas made light work of the sticky mud to open up the Spurs rearguard, although the opening goal owed more to farce than to artistry. In the 20th minute Scottish international goalkeeper Bill Brown made a hash of collecting a 50-yard free kick from Matt Woods. He allowed it to slip through his hands and over his shoulder and it bounced against a post and into the net.

It took Spurs only nine minutes to draw level with a marvellous goal from Cliff Jones. The Welsh left-winger drew the Blackburn defence towards him before flicking the ball with the outside of his foot past the outstretched arms of Harry Leyland. Spurs almost made it 2-1 shortly afterwards but Bobby Smith's hooked shot cannoned off the bar.

Instead, four minutes before half-time, it was Blackburn who went further ahead. Douglas dribbled to the byline before pulling the ball back to Louis Bimpson, keeping his place in the starting line-up after the loss of Vernon. He gave Brown no chance.

The away side might have finished off the tie after 61 minutes but Dougan's drive was deflected onto the angle of the bar with Brown a relieved man. However, eight minutes later Douglas again skipped around left-back Ron Henry and slipped the ball inside to Dougan, who astutely squared it across the face of the goal for Bimpson to apply the finishing touch to the tie.

After that only the woodwork and desperate Spurs defending prevented Blackburn from adding to their total, such that William Westall, writing in *The Blackburn Times*, considered that "the second half was almost as one-sided as a recent occasion in which Crewe were involved".

Mick McGrath remembers: "Bryan Douglas could beat people. He wasn't as quick as Tom Finney or Stanley Matthews and if he beat a player they could often recover to get back at him but he'd just beat them again so it didn't matter. He was a good player, was Bryan; loads of talent. We had a good blend in the side as well.

"Bobby Smith at Spurs was a big rough lad, a good centre-forward, he was. Cliff Jones was a good quick clever winger. They were part of a good Spurs side, but there were a lot of good sides at the time. Wolves were a good side. Every match the opposing side had good players. There were no particularly easy games.

The Fifth Round

"At Tottenham that day the pitch was very muddy; lots of pitches were – today they'd call games off as the pitches are perfect these days; it must be good to play on them. The choice of boots was very important in those days as often one half of the pitch might be iced over as the sun hadn't got on that part of the ground because of the stand and the other part of the pitch was all mud. It could be difficult to stand up depending on what boots you'd chosen. Did you put on boots with studs or basketball boots?

"At Spurs, Louis Bimpson got a free kick on the halfway line that I was going to take but Matt Woods said, 'It's very muddy so fuck off,' and he hits this ball halfway between Derek Dougan and Norman and it slid through Brown. It was the bit of luck you need at times.

"I remember that Bobby Smith was going on about what a good side Spurs were to Matt Woods – 'We've beaten you before,' and how they were going to win this and that – and at the end of the game Matt said to him, 'Remind me to send you a Cup final ticket'. I am not someone who gets really excited but after the Spurs game I felt we had a real chance of at least getting to Wembley and winning the FA Cup."

Wolves were at Luton with Geoff Sidebottom in goal, making his FA Cup debut. Malcolm Finlayson had injured himself colliding with a goalpost against Barcelona at the Nou Camp in the first leg of the European Cup quarter-final ten days earlier when Wolves had lost 4-0.

Sidebottom, another from the Wath nursery, faced a Luton Town team languishing at the bottom of the First Division. Only five of the team that had been beaten 2-1 by Nottingham Forest at Wembley the previous May – Ron Baynham, Brendan McNally, Dave Pacey, Billy Bingham and Bob Morton – were playing.

The pitch was very heavy although this could not stop Bobby Mason giving Wolves the lead after only four minutes. Anyone thinking this might be the start of a rout was quickly dissuaded and Gordon Turner might have equalised shortly afterwards, before a drive from Gerry Harris brought a save from Ron Baynham. Harris had become a professional footballer despite there being no football team at his school in Claverley in Shropshire. He did not start playing until he had left school. He began at Bobbington in the Wolverhampton Amateur League before being snapped up by Wolves.

Sidebottom was proving a worthy deputy for Finlayson, diving full length to turn away a splendid shot from John Groves. The keeper also excelled himself in the 28th minute by pushing a shot from Brendan McNally against the post and away for a corner. However, Sidebottom should have conceded shortly afterwards. Bob Morton took advantage of a slip by Bill Slater to take the ball past the goalkeeper, but with the goal unattended he somehow managed to send the ball wide.

With Billy Bingham, later to manage Northern Ireland with distinction, giving Gerry Harris a torrid time there seemed no way Luton would go in at half-time a goal down and when the Irishman sent left winger Ken Hawkes clear four minutes before the interval only Sidebottom stood between him and an equaliser. But Sidebottom was not be beaten and threw himself at the winger's feet to smother the shot.

Less than two minutes after the restart Wolves were rocked when Luton at last grabbed the goal their play deserved. Bingham was again involved, whipping in a dangerous cross that skimmed off Eddie Clamp's head into the path of Turner, whose first time shot hit Slater and deflected wide of Sidebottom. If the goal contained a touch of good fortune Luton were unlucky when Groves saw a shot deflect off Slater and rise just over the bar.

With the tension rising, Bingham and Clamp were called together for a word or two from the referee before Wolves struck a second in the 64th minute. Deeley took a corner he had forced himself and found the diving Mason, whose magnificent header skimmed just inside the post. This time there was no fightback from the home side. Eight minutes later a sublime pass from Broadbent sent Murray dashing clear to beat Baynham and make it 3-1.

"Jimmy Murray was a fine player," says Malcolm Finlayson. "We had a cracking forward line and scored a hundred goals a season for four seasons running. Our manager believed in attacking, with our particular strength being counter-attacking. We had a quick side with good ability on the ball; we were also very fit and powerful – not only did we have a coach/trainer in Joe Gardiner who had played left half for Wolves in the 1939 FA Cup final, but unlike other sides we also had a physical fitness trainer in Frank Morris, a well-known international runner who'd take the players for athletics.

"The club had spent heavily developing a well-equipped training ground but we'd also go out to Brockton in Staffordshire and be forced to run up this hill to keep fit. If you've seen Sean Connery in the desert film *The Hill* you'll have some idea of what this was like.

"Stan Cullis would water the home pitch as he had us so fit that teams couldn't compete physically and a wet pitch would give us a big advantage. Also the ball in those days was heavier than now at 16 ounces and when it got wet it would be even heavier. Today most players can kick it great distances but not in the '50s – you had to have some strength and fitness to do that, especially towards the end of the match."

Wolves' fourth was a fluke. Clamp crossed and the flight deceived Baynham to hit the inside of the far post and enter the net.

Despite a 4-1 win, newspaper reports after the game were largely critical of Wolves' performance. Denis Compton in the *Sunday Express was typical*. In an article headed "Outplayed Wolves are lucky to win", he wrote: "The Wolves are through to the sixth round and this score suggests that they came through comfortably. Well let me say here and now that the greatest injustice was done. Bottom-of-the-table Luton outplayed and even out-generalled the so-called 'giants' of English football for long periods of the game... The Wolves panicked under pressure and on this display I cannot rate high their chances of reaching Wembley. It was only after they had scored two freak goals in three minutes during the second half – and these were against the run of play – that we saw glimpses of what they are capable of producing."

Perhaps not surprisingly, 'Commentator' in the *Express and Star* didn't share Compton's opinion, stating that, in his view, while "Wolves had to work hard they thoroughly deserved the outright victory they so badly needed at Luton... The game was notable for a splendid performance by Mason... Sidebottom did extremely well in his first FA Cup-tie but undoubtedly the defence's star in this game was Slater, who gave a near-classic display despite the cloying mud. There were times when he tackled and brought the ball out as delicately as though he were playing on a hockey-type surface and his use of the ball was really first class."

"Geoff Sidebottom was a good goalkeeper," says Malcolm Finlayson, "and while we were in competition we always enjoyed each other's company. Of course, being a keeper in the 1950s was entirely different compared with today. Nowadays keepers don't dive at forwards' feet; they all wait until they hit the ball, then they try to spread themselves using their arms and legs. In those days the keeper would dive down at the feet of the forward to try to block or grab the ball. You would also get much more challenged for the ball in the air. These days you see keepers complaining if someone jumps close to them. Keepers were expected to be much more robust in the 1950s.

"Also, how many times do you see keepers trying to anticipate a penalty kick by diving one way? Yet about half of the kicks go down the middle of the goal. Back then keepers tried to watch the ball rather than the player and go after the ball had been kicked.

"The ball did fly straighter in those days – the one great disadvantage keepers have these days is that the ball does move in the air. This makes it much more difficult to catch the ball so they are inclined to punch it more. The weight of the ball meant you couldn't kick it to the halfway line, particularly on wet match days as it collected water. These days keepers can kick it into the opposition half fairly easily.

"At free kicks keepers would try and get their defenders out of the way. Take for example a free kick 35 yards out on the right. The opposition player will attempt to bend it to the back post and defenders drop deep to try to head it clear. This makes it difficult for any keeper to come and get the ball as they've got to get in between the attackers and their own defenders. Defenders drop back because they don't have faith in their 'keeper. At Wolves I would insist that the defence stayed on the 18-yard line and tried to play offside so that if the ball was floated over it was my ball. I would make it clear to any defenders that if they got in the way they could expect to get clattered and if they didn't listen they did.

The Fifth Round

"One main advantage, it has to be said, in those days was that defenders could play the ball back and you could pick it up with your hands; keepers today have to be better with controlling the ball with their feet. Despite this I still feel they have it much easier today than 'keepers had it back in the 1950s and I am not convinced they're any better than we were."

Aston Villa, marching away with the Second Division, were also making progress in the FA Cup and they went through into the quarter-finals by winning 2-1 at Port Vale. Even though prices were increased the match attracted a crowd of 50,000, beating by 6,000 the previous record, which had been set in another FA Cup match against Everton five years earlier. The price hike was met by criticism from many fans and newspapers. They raised the price of 4 shillings (20p) standing accommodation to 7 shillings (35p) and seats from 6 shillings (30p) to eight shillings and 6d (40.5p) – happy days!. It was a trend in those days: Vale were following in the footsteps of Liverpool, for their match with Manchester United, and Bradford City, against Burnley, who had also raised prices in anticipation of bumper gates.

Ticket prices and availability were a constant source of controversy throughout much of the 1950s and 1960s, particularly in the latter stages of the FA Cup. Indeed that weekend the *Sunday Express* ran a special feature on events outside White Hart Lane prior to the Spurs v Blackburn match which revealed that 7 shillings tickets were going for £2 10 s (£2.50) with the police doing nothing to move on or arrest dozens of touts.

Despite the general disgruntlement at having to pay more, 40 volunteers had helped groundstaff remove 1,500 tons of snow from the Vale Park pitch, only to discover that a sudden overnight thaw turned the pitch into a swamp, making it almost impossible for the players to pass the ball on the gluey ground. The match became a dull, monotonous slog.

Port Vale's fans forgot how much they had paid when Vic Crowe brought down Harry Poole and right-winger Brian Jackson gave the home side the lead after 35 minutes from the penalty spot. But Villa used the wings to great effect and scored both of their goals through Gerry Hitchens, on 58 minutes, and a Bobby Thomson back header on 84 – both from crosses by Jimmy MacEwan.

Villa's near neighbours West Bromwich Albion were beaten 2-1 at Leicester while Sheffield Wednesday won a fine match at Old Trafford through a dubious penalty awarded when Maurice Setters was penalised for a challenge on inside left John Fantham after 63 minutes. Tom McAnearney converted it. The Owls held out thanks to Ron Springett in goal.

Preston North End beat Brighton 2-1 while Burnley needed a last-gasp equaliser to take Third Division Bradford City back to Turf Moor for a replay. On a mud heap of a pitch Harry Potts' side had started confidently enough but when Derek Stokes broke away with ten minutes remaining to make it 2-0 it seemed that City were going to take another

The Fifth Round

First Division scalp following their third-round 3-0 dismissal of Everton.

But three minutes later John Connelly ran through the home rearguard to make it 2-1 and Burnley threw everything but the kitchen sink at the Bradford defence, leaving only keeper Adam Blacklaw in their own half. With only seconds remaining Brian Pilkington's free kick was touched on to the bar and Connelly spared the First Division side's blushes by pushing the ball into the net.

The Quarter-finals

THE QUARTER-FINAL draw sent Wolves the short distance to play Leicester City at Filbert Street. Having lost the previous two FA Cup encounters against Wolves, including the 1949 final, the Foxes were hoping to make it third time lucky.

Leicester were having a difficult time in their third season back in the First Division following promotion as Division Two Champions at the end of 1956–57. In comparison, Wolves were undefeated in domestic competition in 1960 but had been firmly put in their place in the European Cup quarter-final ten days earlier at Molineux when Barcelona ran off 5-2 victors on the night and 9-2 on aggregate. Sandor Kocsis showed what a truly great player he was by hammering in four goals as Wolves were outclassed.

Those glorious floodlit Molineux nights against foreign opposition that had decorated the 1950s were well and truly over as football accustomed itself to the new decade.

Thankfully, Leicester were no Barcelona, although they did have goalkeeper Gordon Banks, who after just 23 games for Chesterfield had signed for the East Midlands side at a cost of £7,000 in the summer of 1959. Banks, who replaced Dave McLaren, was to have a fantastic career in football, making 73 England

The Quarter-finals

international appearances including, of course, when the World Cup was won in 1966.

With Finlayson still injured, Sidebottom retained his place in the Wolves goal while Barry Stobart was making his FA Cup debut. At Old Trafford the week before the young forward had played his first senior game and headed home a cross from another debutant, Gerry Mannion, in a 2-0 victory against Manchester United.

According to Sir Bobby Charlton: "To beat Wolves, their big strong defenders and quick and skilful forwards dressed in gold, you had to do so much more than merely play well. You had to function completely as a team."

George Showell retained his place in the side at right-back. He had played the previous three matches after coming into the side against Luton Town in the league game played three days after the FA Cup fifth-round tie. Showell's chance came after Harris was injured and to accommodate him Cullis moved Eddie Stuart to left-back where, according to 'Commentator', "he did not exactly look happy but that did not warrant the shocking treatment he received from the crowd. There is nothing worse than a player being pilloried by the home spectators and it certainly did not help Stuart."

After the abuse Cullis announced he would be resting the South African for that weekend's derby with West Bromwich Albion but "would not enlarge on the situation." It later transpired that Stuart had been singled out by some spectators because of his nationality. South Africa was in turmoil under the apartheid regime and during the first few months of 1960 internal resistance had been met by fierce suppression that peaked on March 21st in Sharpeville, where 69 people were murdered by the police.

Stuart recalled: "The events in South Africa had nothing to do with me. I was never a racist but I started receiving letters at the shop I owned in town criticising me for what was happening. When I turned out at the Molineux against Luton Town in the league I was booed every time I touched the ball, even though I captained the side that day.

"As a result of this unfortunate situation our manager, Stan Cullis, decided to rest me. My place was then taken by George Showell, who's now a friend of mine as we live a short distance from each other in Wrexham. Bill Slater was made captain and he and George both played extremely well from then on.

"Stan Cullis very rarely changed a winning team and consequently I was unable to get my place back. A season that started so memorably finished on a very sad note, because while I made in into the 12 for Wembley there were no subs in those days so I had no chance of ever getting on. I sat on the bench all afternoon."

The quarter-final at Leicester's Filbert Street ground was played in blustery conditions before a capacity 39,000 crowd, with home fans hooting in the first few minutes when Wolves employed the offside trap. Frank McLintock, later to win the FA

The Quarter-finals

Cup with Arsenal in 1971 as part of the double-winning team, was then denied an opening goal by a fine diving save from Sidebottom.

However, in the 11th minute Wolves took the lead with a simple goal. Clamp sent a pass through the middle to Peter Broadbent, who, fully utilising the space around him, advanced to the edge of the penalty area to drive the ball past Banks. Sidebottom then kept the scores level by diving bravely at the feet of Jimmy Walsh, requiring treatment after the ball was scrambled away.

Wolves struck for a second time just before the half hour. A free kick from Clamp was hooked back into the goalmouth by Stobart and Leicester left-back Len Chalmers headed it over his own goalkeeper.

Leicester managed to get back into the game ten minutes later when ex-Wolves player Tommy McDonald nipped in front of Bill Slater to drive Ken Leek's lob into the net from just a couple of yards. Stobart could have made the game safe for the away side but drove his shot just over the bar before Sidebottom was again down and injured after Ken Leek clattered into him.

With Leicester pushing forward in search of an equaliser, Wolves' ability to play a counter-attacking style should have seen the League Champions finish off the match. But Stobart, again, and Deeley wasted opportunities. Late in the game Mason hit the post but Stan Cullis's men were grateful to Sidebottom, who made two fine flying saves, from a header by

Walsh and a cross from McDonald. The victory took Wolves to their tenth FA Cup semi-final.

The match had been a hard-fought affair that often threatened to get out of control and the press slated it. Typical of the comments were those of Ken Jones in the *Daily Mirror*: "This match was soccer at its lowest. I am convinced that the FA Cup, British Football's No 1 glamour competition, is becoming the game's worst advert. For the whole 90 minutes it was crash-bang soccer with hardly one breath of imagination or intelligence to break the monotony of crash tackles and aimless passes."

Others followed suit, including Peter Lorenzo in the *News Chronicle*: "This was spoiling soccer at its worst, with victory rightly going to the better spoilers."

Gordon Banks did not agree. Writing in *Banksy: My Autobiography* more than 40 years later, he declared: "It was a classic quarter-final full of cut and thrust."

Six of the 1960 Leicester side against Wolves – Banks, Chalmers, McLintock, Appleton, Cheeseborough and Walsh – were in the team that lost 2-0 to Spurs in the FA Cup final a year later. Banks, McLintock and Appleton also played for the club in the 1963 FA Cup final when they again finished with losers' medals after a 3-1 defeat by Manchester United. Leicester later made it an unfortunate 1960s 'treble' when they lost to Manchester City in the 1969 final, by which time Peter Shilton had replaced Gordon Banks.

The Quarter-finals

Ken Jones made Slater Wolves' man of the match with nine out of 10, equal to Willie Cunningham for Leicester. Jones later voted for the Wolves centre-half in the Football Writers' Player of the Year Award because "I had seen how his career from an amateur had developed and he had a fine season in 1959–60. He was a solid, hard-working player admired by everyone who played and watched football at that time. He was also one of the few England players to do well in Sweden at the 1958 World Cup."

Jones, from a famous footballing family, had been a professional footballer himself with Swansea, Southend and Gravesend before injury ended his career and a trial with the *Mirror* saw him taken on permanently as a journalist.

His cousin Cliff Jones played 58 times for Wales and was one of the stars of the famous double-winning 1961 Spurs side, for which he made the first of three successful FA Cup final appearances. Ken Jones's uncle was Brynmor Jones, a Molineux favourite whose transfer to Arsenal just prior to the start of World War II almost caused a riot despite the world record fee of £14,000 Wolves were paid for his services.

Blackburn's quarter-final reward for their thrilling White Hart Lane victory was a tie at Turf Moor against local rivals Burnley, who were chasing the championship as well as the FA Cup. But before this local derby could take place Burnley had to win their replay with Bradford City. It proved a formality as

Burnley duly walloped the Yorkshiremen 5-0 at Turf Moor.

Not surprisingly, the Blackburn encounter captured the imagination of the east Lancashire public – the two clubs still have a rivalry that matches any from Glasgow, the North East or north London. It was all-ticket with the capacity set at 54,000 and tickets with a face value of 3 shillings exchanged hands for at least treble that outside the ground beforehand.

Mick McGrath recalls the excitement: "After the Spurs game I felt we had a chance and when the draw came out and we would play Burnley if they won their replay then the whole town was abuzz. People were asking for tickets, and 'Do you fancy your chances?'

"In those days teams like Burnley and Blackburn had a chance of keeping hold of their good players because the maximum wage meant that someone moving still got paid the same, although people did move because it was rumoured they might get some money under the counter."

When the maximum wage was ended for footballers in 1961 it stood at £20 a week. Female sewing machinists at the Elgin manufacturing company near Burnley in the early '60s were earning just over £10 a week. On his wages, a footballer would have struggled to buy a car as Loxhams of Blackburn at the start of 1960 were selling a 1958 two-door Morris-Minor for £550 and 1959 Wolseleys at £675. It was hardly surprising that footballers, watched by thousands, were threatening to strike in order to push up their wages as well as end the practice whereby clubs could refuse players' requests to move to another club.

Blackburn and Burnley had met three times in the FA Cup, including the previous season when goals from Jimmy Robson and Jimmy McIlroy against a single effort from Peter Dobing had seen Burnley home at Turf Moor. That had been a game with more than its fair share of thrills, but it was nothing like the 1960 match staged on March 12th. It produced one of the greatest FA Cup comebacks, sparked off by a penalty decision that still rankles with older Burnley fans and ex-players.

As so often seems to happen, the teams met in the league the weekend before the cup-tie, with both, despite Burnley gunning for the title, playing cautiously in a match described by the *Blackburn Times* as being "one of the most concentrated efforts in concealment since Hitler masked his real intentions when he met Chamberlain at Munich." Who said papers today have a tendency to exaggerate! Burnley won by a single goal to maintain their First Division challenge.

Both sides were at full strength for the cup-tie with Blackburn again choosing Douglas at inside left and Bimpson on the right wing. This meant there was the direct contest between Jimmy McIlroy and Bryan Douglas to whet the appetite. Both sets of fans were adamant that their man was the better, with many believing that whoever came out on top in this personal battle would probably win the war.

Douglas is still idolised at Ewood Park while McIlroy was king of Turf Moor and remains an iconic figure in the town. One of the stands at Turf Moor is named after him.

He'd made his debut as a 19-year-old in October 1950 and not only was he an outstanding passer of the ball, he also had the ability to beat players and he scored goals: 131 in 497 first team appearances. This made him one of the outstanding players of his generation.

But in spite of all the talent on show, the first half was poor, the cagey pattern of the previous weekend's game carried on into the cup-tie. Burnley were on top early on but although they pressed hard it was still goalless at half-time with few chances having been created.

When the game restarted, the home team, inspired by McIlroy, poured forward. What was astonishing was that Burnley's talisman was not fully fit. He had been suffering for some time from a thigh muscle injury but Burnley needed him as they pressed Wolves and Spurs for the title.

Just three minutes had gone in the second period when the Irishman picked open the Blackburn defence. Pilkington controlled the crossfield pass before blasting the ball past Leyland.

Louis Bimpson forced a flying save from Adam Blacklaw and then shot wide from an even better position. But Blackburn's momentum proved

The Quarter-finals

illusory. Just nine minutes after taking the lead Burnley doubled it. From close to the byline McIlroy, in what he states in his autobiography was one of his favourite places on the field, shimmied past two defenders before picking out Ray Pointer, who knocked home one of the 23 league and FA Cup goals he scored that season.

With this two-goal cushion it seemed a place in the semi-final for the first time since 1947 was assured for Harry Potts and his team. Almost immediately Burnley grabbed a third.

Before the match Burnley had felt that a long pass over the head of Dave Whelan would give John Connelly the chance to use his blistering pace and when Jimmy Adamson hit just such a ball the winger left two startled defenders in his wake. Leyland plunged at his feet but the England winger coolly lifted the ball over him and into the net. It was game, set and match, surely?

One can only hope that no Blackburn fans decided on an early trip home. Had they left they would have missed a remarkable comeback although initially it seemed Burnley would further extend their lead.

The rivalry between the two sets of supporters was such that Burnley wanted to score more goals. With hindsight they might have been better to have shut up shop and run down the clock. Had they done that they might have gone on to become the first side in the twentieth century to record the league and FA Cup 'double'. Still, at 3-0 up, what on earth could go wrong?

But the key moment in the match came after 70 minutes. Peter Dobing had rarely featured as an attacking threat and his shot appeared to be heading well wide only for the ball to hit defender Alex Elder's foot and rise up and strike his hand.

To a supporter it was either a clear penalty or a travesty, depending on which club you followed, but independent match reports expressed surprise that referee Jack Hunt pointed to the penalty spot. Bryan Douglas converted the kick to make it 3-1. Surely this would prove to be just a consolation?

Not so, for within a minute the home fans had reason to wonder. The Burnley defence relaxed as Douglas appeared to mess up a free kick. The apparent disarray was a ruse; Douglas touched the ball to Dobing, who hit a reasonable, but not unstoppable shot, but Blacklaw seemed unsighted and it was 3-2.

There was still quarter of an hour left and the mood inside Turf Moor had changed. Blackburn were in the ascendant and their fans were buoyant. Desperately Burnley tried to cling on, having given up any ideas of scoring a fourth in order to protect Adam Blacklaw in goal. The tension was growing as the final whistle moved ever closer. Blackburn, of course, had fashioned an undeserved equaliser against Blackpool in the fourth round – could they do it again?

The answer was yes. A Matt Woods free kick was only half cleared and when Ronnie Clayton hacked it back towards the goal it ricocheted perfectly into the path of Mick McGrath, the man who had scored the equaliser against Blackpool. It was a difficult chance – Blacklaw and two defenders close to the line had to be beaten – but the Irish international got a slice of luck, literally. His shot sliced off his boot and the ball rocketed into the net to make it 3-3. There were just four minutes left.

Blackburn weren't finished, and might even have won the game in the remaining minutes had either Dobing or Dougan shown McGrath's composure by bringing better placed colleagues into play as Burnley's defence evaporated. It was a draw but at the final whistle only one group of players and supporters were celebrating. Burnley might have still been in the 1960 FA Cup but who really believed the replay wouldn't go Blackburn's way?

Even fifty years later Jimmy McIlroy feels the hurt. "It was a disappointing result. There was no way Alex Elder tried to handle the ball or gain any benefit from handling it. The ball hit the ground and it must have hit a bump or something and it did hit his hand but it was never intentional and should never have been a penalty. Alex was in tears afterwards; he couldn't face going out as he put all our misfortune on his shoulders. I still prefer to blame a gentleman with a whistle called Mr Hunt."

The view from the other side was put by McIlroy's opposite number, Bryan Douglas. "Alex Elder went for the ball with his arms up and the ball ricocheted and hit him on the arm, just above the elbow on the inside of the arm. If we'd been winning say 3-0 I'm not sure we'd have got it. I've seen them turned down but it threw us a chance. I'd seen Burnley's keeper Adam Blacklaw save one a few weeks earlier and I sent the ball to his left and it went in.

"The second goal I remember very well. It came from practising on the training ground. We'd copied the idea from another side – I can't remember who. We went to pretend we'd buggered up the free-kick in the hope that the other side would be taken off guard and then we could exploit that.

"I pretended to take it and everyone ran; I then ran and they stopped – everyone including the Burnley players was laughing at our stupidity. Then I tapped it to Peter Dobing, who was fully aware of what was happening, and he cracked it past the keeper to make it 3-2. After Mick McGrath equalised we actually had a chance to win the match in the last minute when Dougan was clear on the left-hand side and he only had to square it to me. I was standing in the clear just yards out. The keeper was moving out to block him but Dougan preferred to shoot and the ball cannoned off the keeper's legs.

"Burnley had a good side; their forward line was something special in Connolly, McIlroy, Pointer, Robson and Pilkington. The rivalry was intense even in those days and the games were often not that great. Since I finished I've met a number of Burnley players and I've found them to be human. To be honest the rivalry is a bit unhealthy.

"I definitely feel that football in those days was more exciting. There were more mistakes, but there was also more goalmouth action. I am not saying it was more skilful but in those days wingers and players tried to take on the full backs and get to the byline. These days you never see a player leave the full back for dead; at times today the games can be like a game of chess."

Mick McGrath remembers: "We were dead and buried at Burnley, when we got that dubious penalty. It was only when we got back in the game at 3-2 that I ventured forward as I was a defensive wingback. I remember the equaliser very well even after all this time. Adam Blacklaw, the Burnley keeper, was on his knees and when the ball came to me I just hit it – my shot was sliced and this was why Adam went down one way and the ball went the other into the corner – it was a good miskick!

"All of us were overjoyed. I was surrounded by the other players, which was very unusual for those days as normally when you scored you got a little tap off one or two players who then ran back to the halfway line. But after being three-nil down this was something a bit special. So the players sort of swamped me. From where he was watching Dally Duncan couldn't tell who'd scored and as we went off he asked, 'Who scored the equaliser?' It was the best goal I scored for Rovers, but I did only score 12!"

Fifty Years On

The replay

The replay failed to provide the quality or excitement of the first match as extra-time goals from Dobing and MacLeod put Blackburn into their 16th FA Cup semi-final. They deserved to win and reach a second semi-final at Maine Road in two years, their third in nine years.

With Whelan and Bray close marking Burnley's wingers Connelly and Pilkington, Burnley struggled to gather any forward thrust, especially as their potential match-winner McIlroy did not enjoy as much possession as in the first hour or so of the first game. Although pressed back for much of the game, Burnley were never out of it, and nearly snatched the winner with five minutes of normal time remaining when only a great save from Leyland stopped Connelly from scoring.

The opening goal came in the 13th minute of extra time after Dougan flicked on a free kick from Douglas for Dobing to steer the ball through a crowd of Burnley players in and around the six-yard box, a goal much like that scored by McGrath at Turf Moor. The goal was reward for Dobing's persistence as in the first half of the game he'd been denied by two fine saves from Blacklaw, while in the second only a flying block by John Angus had prevented the Blackburn inside right opening the scoring.

Any hopes that Burnley, and their considerable following, had of the game being rescued ended when, with two minutes of extra time remaining, Bimpson headed on a long throw from Clayton, and MacLeod, anticipating superbly, dashed beyond an exhausted Burnley defence to head the ball past Blacklaw and spark a minor pitch invasion by a section of the ecstatic home following. There was another a minute later which had to be cleared by the police to allow the referee to play the final 30 seconds.

Writing in the *Blackburn Times*, William Westall again praised Douglas, who in his view "proved himself the outstanding craftsman by his diligent foraging, grafting and subtle moves". However, in his view, Rovers won "primarily through a truly magnificent halfback line of Clayton, Woods and McGrath: every man a giant".

But it was McGrath who particularly caught his eye. He described him as "the finest player on the field: a footballing tiger, so relentless, so mercilessly dominant that Burnley seemed almost to be physically afraid of him. He not only played McIlroy right out of the picture, but also was often a sixth forward apparently intent on winning the game himself. I have never seen a player so uplifted by the Cup atmosphere."

Matt Woods reckons extra time should not have been necessary. "In the replay we should have won it in the first 90 minutes."

Not surprisingly, Jimmy McIroy disagrees. "Looking back even now I still feel we could, and should have reached the semi-final… if not the Cup final. Rovers scored five times against us but none came from a thoughtful, skilfully executed attack."

Sheffield Wedensday triumphed 2-0 in their quarter-final which was even more of a derby than Blackburn v Burnley, being that it was against their city rivals United, while Aston Villa also won 2-0, beating Preston North End. Sadly it meant that Tom Finney would end his career without ever winning an FA Cup winner's medal.

Villa's victory meant another derby in the semi-final as they were to meet Wolves at The Hawthorns, home of West Bromwich Albion, Wolves' biggest rivals, who were also, of course, local to Villa.

The Semi-finals

ONLY ONE semi-final had ever been staged at The Hawthorns and that had been 58 years before, when Sheffield United and Derby County played out the first of two 1-1 draws, the replay taking place at Molineux before the Blades triumphed at the third attempt at the City Ground, Nottingham.

This was the fifth time Wolves and Aston Villa had met in the Cup and Villa enjoyed a 3-1 advantage. But in 1960 Villa were in the Second Division and although they were to go up as champions Wolves were a First Divison colossus. And it was Wolves who imposed themselves at the start with wing halves Eddie Clamp and Ron Flowers taking control to play Bobby Thomson and Ron Wylie, Villa's inside forwards, out of the game. This had the effect of forcing danger man Peter McParland to wander from the left wing looking for the ball.

Yet Villa were not entirely without hope. Centre-forward Gerry Hitchens gave Bill Slater some anxious moments, using his speed and strength to search for goalscoring opportunities.

It was, however, no surprise when Wolves took the lead. With 32 minutes on the clock, Peter Broadbent's quick throw was returned to him by 19-year-old Gerry Mannion, making his Cup debut. Shimmying one way and then the other, Broadbent threw the

Second Division side's defence into total confusion before arching a near-perfect cross which allowed centre-forward Jimmy Murray to hit the ball with pace and precision. This brought out a fine diving save by Villa keeper Nigel Sims, once of Wolves, but he was left sprawled on the ground as Norman Deeley raced to crash the ball into the net for the game's only goal.

Malcolm Finlayson remembers: "Little Norman was a tiny wee chap at about 5′ 2″ but he was very quick and had great feet. He had a great partnership with Peter Broadbent and they were always interpassing the ball and interchanging positions. Norman could and did create space around him in which to play. Peter Broadbent was also a very good player. Jimmy Murray was a good player with two good feet. He would always look for the open space and like Norman always seemed to have room to play, allowing him to look up."

Newspaper reports were as one in selecting Broadbent as the game's outstanding player, with Bill Slater also singled out for praise along with right-back George Showell and the new man Mannion, for whom big things were being predicted by some journalists.

Deeley revealed many years later that he had not expected to play after Stan Cullis had accused him the previous day of putting money on Villa to win. Deeley responded by telling Cullis to leave him out before going despondently for a few drinks. He was therefore surprised when he saw his name included

The Semi-finals

in the team, only this time at number 11, Des Horne being dropped. Deeley was determined to prove his manager wrong and when he saw him the day after the semi-final back at Molineux he couldn't resist saying, "I threw the game then, didn't I?" Deeley was fully aware, though, that Cullis had simply employed an unusual motivational technique.

Villa might have equalised shortly after the goal but McParland, generally well marshalled by Showell, was forced by alert defending into pushing his shot into the side netting after his run took him clear of the rest of Villa's forwards.

George Showell recalls: "Peter McParland was the big star – he eventually came to the Wolves – and I had a fairly good game to keep him quiet that day. You can never tell before you step on the field whether everything will go for you. I had to work hard to make it as a footballer, especially at Wolves as they had such a big staff and you only had a contract for 12 months. You had to wait to see whether you'd be retained, which was always a worry. "The Wolves side had some good players. Peter Broadbent was one. He had unbelievable skill. He was the first player I ever saw trap the ball with his backside. Ron Flowers was excellent in midfield. Eddie Clamp, who played in front of me, was another international. He was brilliant to play with – when you were under pressure he was a big help."

Malcolm Finlayson, who had been absent for the previous two cup games, was determined not to miss out on the semi-final. So much so that he admits he was prepared to gamble on his fitness. "I missed Luton and Leicester but I played through the pain barrier against Villa as I felt that if I missed the game and Wolves went on to Wembley I might not get a place in the final.

"Funnily enough, I found out later that the Villa keeper Nigel Sims, a good friend of mine, had a similar injury and had taken a similar decision. I missed a number of matches after hurting my shoulder in Barcelona, but I was determined to play at Wembley and so I played at The Hawthorns. Obviously, if it had been impossible to play I wouldn't have but it was a bit of a gamble. I didn't have an injection to deaden the pain, which I saw other players have during my career. I saw them a few hours afterwards and they would be in a lot of pain so it must have damaged them."

Fortunately, Finlayson had relatively little to do, being extended only twice. First the big goalkeeper, whose appearance ended reserve keeper Geoff Sidebottom's nine-match run – a sequence which contained seven victories and only one defeat – was forced in the first half to make a diving save to stop a shot from Jimmy McEwan; then 12 minutes from the end he found himself facing Bobby Thomson. It was a crucial moment and one Malcolm Finlayson remembers as he still has the scars to show from what happened next!

"Bobby, an ex-Wolves player, was clever. Wolves were known for pushing up to leave attackers offside. We'd push up to the halfway line; it would annoy the hell out of the opponents' fans when we played away. The opposing player would push the ball through to their forwards and we'd get an offside flag. This day Bobby pushed the ball through and went after it himself. I met him on the 18-yard line and dived at his feet. Out of frustration he raked his studs down the inside of my thigh and even today when I see him I tell him I've still got the scars to show from his tackle. He says it was an accident. It wasn't and today he would be sent off but in those days you could and did expect such things to happen as it was a much harder game than it is today."

Villa keeper Nigel Sims was "naturally disappointed. I had hoped to return to Wembley after playing there in the 1957 final, but Wolves had some fine players. I actually made my First Division debut for Wolves at The Hawthorns when I was called up as the understudy to Bert Williams for a match on October 18th 1952. I thought it was unlikely I'd keep Bert out of the side as he was the England custodian at the time and he was a really excellent keeper. I did, however, make another 12 appearances that season so I was hopeful of a long career at Wolves. I played the first five league games of the next season but I only got three games in 1954–55 and five the next season. So when I got the chance to move to Villa I jumped at it.

"It also got me away from Stan Cullis. He was, of course, a great manager, and I wouldn't like anybody to think otherwise. But he was horrible; nobody liked him. I even saw him tell the directors off, including

John Ireland, the man who finally sacked him. He would talk to people like dirt – I suppose it was just a different era.

"When I played at Wembley against Manchester United in the 1957 final it was the greatest day in my football career. We were up against a very good side that was going for the double but on the day we managed to win 2-1 and I virtually floated up the stairs to collect my winner's medal. Even now, more than 50 years later, you get people coming up to you and shaking your hand. It remains a truly marvellous memory.

"Looking back to my time as a footballer you do realise you were badly paid but at the time I and Malcolm Finlayson, a great friend of mine, used to say to each other just how marvellous it was to play at places such as Old Trafford and Molineux. I came from a very small mining community and to play football professionally was a dream and one I enjoyed, especially when I moved to Villa and obtained regular first team football."

Steve Gordos recalls: "The semi-final was really special as we played the Villa and it was at The Hawthorns. I recall that Malcolm Finlayson had a very good game and saved Wolves once or twice. He had a hard act to follow in England keeper Bert Williams and it was a shame he never played for his country, Scotland, at least once. But in those days the Scottish League wasn't too keen to play the 'Anglos' so he missed out. Malcolm was very good at getting down at an attacking player's feet to grab

The Semi-finals

the ball. He also had good positional sense, which often meant that he didn't have to make saves."

Having seen their team, then in the Second Division, lose to Bolton and Newcastle United respectively in their last two semi-finals, the Blackburn Rovers fans were hoping it would be a case of third time lucky. Standing in their way would be Sheffield Wednesday, rated with Wolves as joint favourites.

Both teams had reasons to treat Maine Road with trepidation. Wednesday had lost to Preston North End there in the 1954 semi-final while Blackburn went down to Bolton in 1958, a match Matt Woods still feels Rovers "were a bit unfortunate to lose".

He says: "When you get to the semi-final there's a bit of added pressure as it's every footballer's dream to play at Wembley, or rather it was because it's been devalued with the number of games played there now. To play at Wembley was something special. I'd been down once previously with Everton to watch the 1954 final between West Brom and Preston and I was determined to play my part in beating Wednesday."

After only one win in their previous six games form was against Blackburn, especially as Wednesday had won nine and lost just one of their previous twelve matches. Yet if there's one thing any fan knows about the FA Cup it's that form can easily be overturned at the semi-final stage. Rovers had history on their side, having beaten Wednesday in the last four before. True, that victory was back in 1882 – but with the gods firmly on their side, how could the Lancastrians not prove successful?

And it was Blackburn who started confidently. Ron Springett, a non-playing member of the England World Cup winning squad six years later, was forced to make three great saves before Rovers took the lead after 12 minutes. As Wednesday defenders appealed for offside, Derek Dougan raced away on to a through ball from Bryan Douglas to crack the ball past Springett.

Wednesday piled forward, only to come up against a Blackburn rearguard in obdurate mood. They restricted the Owls to a series of shots from distance, which Harry Leyland had no trouble in collecting. As a result Blackburn led 1-0 at half-time.

However, Wednesday showed their intentions as soon as the second half began and Derek Wilkinson shot just wide after cutting in from the right wing. Seven minutes after the interval Alan Finney had the ball in the net after Leyland had parried another shot from Wilkinson. But as the jubilant Wednesday forwards raced away and the Wednesday fans celebrated the referee disallowed the goal – Finney was offside.

Blackburn weathered the Wednesday onslaught and Dougan put them further ahead after 71 minutes, beating Peter Swan to Ally MacLeod's through ball.

Though 2-0 down the Yorkshire side wouldn't surrender and six minutes later Tom McAnearney's free kick was headed powerfully across goal and into the net by Johnny Fantham to make it 2-1. Ironically

The Semi-finals

the goal came when Wednesday were playing with only ten men, Keith Ellis having been stretchered off to receive treatment.

But the comeback was not completed and when the whistle sounded Blackburn Rovers had made it through to their second FA Cup Wembley final, 32 years after the first.

According to Alec Johnson of the *Sunday Express*, "it was a semi-final of crashing tackles, of bungled chances, of thrill upon thrill and at times of brilliance."

Matt Woods recalls: "I was delighted to beat Sheffield Wednesday. I remember Harry Leyland, who's the bravest keeper I've seen, making one or two cracking saves. On a one-on-one Leyland was great as he'd go down bravely to grab the ball. I didn't feel any great sympathy for Wednesday as no one had any sympathy for us when we lost. We came under a lot of pressure towards the end but there are no easy games."

"Knowing I was going to be playing at Wembley ranks alongside the news I was to be capped for Ireland as my greatest thrill in football," says Mick McGrath. "I played for Home Farm in Dublin – Man United came in first but that never worked out. I was delighted when Johnny Carey from Blackburn approached me to join after he'd seen the 1954 Irish Cup final.

"I came over with Charlie Wade. I had been out of Ireland once, which was for a match with the Irish Youth side in Germany, and that was it. Charlie and I arrived on August 24th 1954, on a day when Blackburn were at home to Derby. When we got dropped off outside the ground in a taxi the commissionaire, who controlled entry to the main entrance, said to us: 'Go upstairs, sit down at the back of the stand and keep quiet.' We did as we were told; you did in those days.

"Afterwards Johnny Carey came and sorted out our digs, in which we shared a double bed: that brought us down to earth. I signed forms at £9 a week, a pound less in the summer, and I had a £25 signing-on fee, half of which I sent to my mother. I used to send my mam £2 a week and also paid £3 for my digs. Our family needed the money as there were seven kids. I can remember the time when the family had no money at all.

"In the semi-final Harry Leyland had a great game, a blinder, making a lot of good saves. I was picking up Bobby Craig and Matt was picking up the big lad Fantham and, typical Matt, he was offering him a cup final ticket at the end! Mind you, as he'd already offered Bobby Smith tickets after we beat them in the fifth round I'm not sure he had any left."

Derek Dougan also offered cup final tickets to his marker Peter Swan at the end of the match, an offer which Swan didn't take kindly. He responded by kicking his opponent up the backside. It was as near as he had got to Dougan all afternoon, the man from Northern Ireland having played his finest game in Blackburn Rovers colours. Signed from Portsmouth to replace veteran campaigner Tom Johnston, Dougan's off-the-field antics often proved more newsworthy than what he did on the pitch.

The Semi-finals

Sir Bobby Charlton remembers Bryan Douglas and Ronnie Clayton: "Bryan Douglas was a wonderfully clever little winger who later developed his craft superbly when he moved inside. Ronnie Clayton wasn't in the class of Johnny Haynes as a creative player, but he did see the whole picture of the game, and he wasn't afraid to put his foot in if things turned rough. He was always ready to fight for his team.'"

Meanwhile, in an interesting aside, considering what happened, Roy Peskett of the *Sunday Express* interviewed Dally Duncan after the semi-final. The manager expressed his disappointment that in the after-dinner speeches following Luton Town's defeat at Wembley no one had mentioned his part in building the team which reached the 1959 final, Duncan having left Luton in October 1958.

"People have such short memories," said Duncan, a cup winner with Derby in 1946. "What a wonderful thing it is for our chairman, Mr Norman Forbes, whose four-year-term is up this year – promotion, the youngsters won the FA Youth Cup last year and now Wembley. Blackburn is a grand club, they have a fine set of directors, and the players have done all that has been asked of them. I do not regret leaving Luton at all."

Leading up to the Final

FOLLOWING THE semi-finals, the players had six weeks to wait before they ran out at Wembley, and they had very different priorities. Wolves were aiming to capture a third consecutive league title, a feat achieved only by Huddersfield in the 1920s, Arsenal in the 1930s and Manchester United twice in more recent years.

A title victory would also open up the opportunity of Wolves recording only the third ever double of League and Cup victories in the same season – only Preston North End in 1888–89 and Aston Villa in 1896–97 had done it before.

Blackburn, meanwhile with 31 points from 33 matches, thought they could relax, knowing they were unlikely to be relegated, especially as they beat Chelsea 1-0 at home following the semi-final. Disappointingly the crowd was only 15,832.

On the same night Wolves roared back into League action by walloping rivals Burnley 6-1 at Molineux with all five forwards scoring. Mannion, playing in place of Deeley, grabbed two. But the man of the match was Broadbent, whose passing tore Harry Potts' men apart. The result meant that Wolves moved within a point of Spurs at the top of the table.

Three days later Wolves travelled to Elland Road with Mannion knocking home all three goals. The

Leading up to the Final

youngster added to his growing reputation by scoring again as Wolves beat West Ham 5-0 before 48,086 at Molineux to go top. The match had been moved from the Saturday to the Monday evening as Slater, Flowers and Broadbent were playing against Scotland at Hampden Park in the Home Championships.

This postponement created a precedent as before then clubs with players chosen for England were obliged to release them yet still play their scheduled fixtures. The rule did not apply to non-England players and that weekend Spurs refused to release Brown, Mackay and White to play for Scotland. Captaining the England side was Ronnie Clayton. The match finished 1-1 and the crowd was 129,193!

That weekend's sports pages contained a number of pieces suggesting that when he retired from playing Bill Slater was in line to replace Walter Winterbottom as England manager. We know now that Jimmy Adamson refused the offer before Alf Ramsey took it on. Even fifty years later Slater is unwilling to comment.

The West Ham victory put Wolves on top but their title hopes suffered a blow when Broadbent was injured in training. Although his replacement, the young South African Cliff Durandt, did his best, Wolves returned from St James' Park on Easter Saturday beaten by a single Len White goal. This dropped them to second, below Spurs and level on points with third-placed Burnley, who had a game in hand. When Nottingham Forest

Fifty Years On

were beaten 3-1 two days later the pendulum again swung in Wolves' favour. Spurs had lost 1-0 at home to Chelsea while Burnley fell 2-1 at Leicester. Wolves' third goal took Cullis's side, for the third consecutive season, on to 100 league goals, a magnificent record and one they repeated the following season. Ironically the century was achieved through an own goal scored by Nottingham Forest's Joe McDonald.

And the victory was not without its downside as Broadbent, Deeley and Flowers were injured and forced to sit out the return match at the City Ground the following day. In the circumstances a goalless draw was not a bad result, especially as in the first half Jim Iley missed a penalty for Forest. Fortunately all three were passed fit for the home match with Spurs on St George's Day.

Before the match the top of the table read:

Wolves	40 games	52 points
Spurs	40 games	49 points
Burnley	38 games	49 points

The result and the performance was to have major consequences for both the team and one player in particular: Bobby Mason, who had missed only five first team games that season. The Londoners won 3-1 with goals from Bobby Smith, Dave Mackay and Cliff Jones being countered only by a strike from Peter Broadbent.

With Burnley earning a 1-1 draw at Blackpool the table now read:

Leading up to the Final

Wolves	1 game left	52 points
Spurs	1 game left	51 points
Burnley	3 games left	50 points

It was a considerable blow to Wolves' double chances and the comments of Maurice Smith in the following day's *Sunday People* were typical: "This was the day when the Wolves' hopes of that double died. Because their forwards died."

In the same paper ex-England, Blackburn and Arsenal winger Joe Hulme used his column to advise Cullis to "have a few words with those inside forwards. They did not close enough. There was no sense of urgency."

The inside-forwards were Broadbent and Mason, yet by all accounts Broadbent had played well enough.

Consolation for some Wolves fans, 8,500 of them, came with the knowledge they had been lucky in the club's FA Cup final ticket ballot and would be joining season ticket holders at Wembley in two weeks' time. The club had received 32,000 applications and among the fortunate 25 per cent were Paul Bowyer and German-born Fräulein Ute Thieme, from Hanover, who had a second reason to celebrate as they had been married the morning before the Spurs match. The couple had met when the bridegroom was on National Service in Germany.

In midweek Burnley recorded a single-goal victory against Birmingham City at St Andrew's to put themselves in a great position to win the title. They were now level on points with Wolves and still had a game in hand. They had been given the chance to play their final league game on the Monday after Wolves and Spurs had completed their league programmes, something that would not be allowed today.

Meanwhile Blackburn were taking it easy – rather too easy, in fact. With only two points from six matches they had slipped uncomfortably close to the relegation trap door. When 21st-placed Leeds United made the relatively short trip to Ewood Park for the penultimate match of the season Blackburn were lying 18th. With 35 points they were only three points better off than the Yorkshiremen. So there was a real danger that defeat would see them run out at Wembley as a Second Division club. Thus far only Manchester City in 1926 had reached the cup final and been relegated in the same season. Since then Leicester City in 1969 and Middlesbrough in 1997 have followed suit.

The match with Leeds was intense. There was therefore relief among the home fans in a poor crowd of 19,295 when Roy Isherwood, playing on the right wing, scored twice and provided the cross from which Dougan headed the winner. Isherwood's finest performance in a Blackburn shirt was unlikely to win him a place in the Wembley line-up but, at least, it seemed that if one of the Rovers front men wasn't fit he could be called upon to do his bit. Rovers, having collected only eight points from their final 19 matches, finished 17th with 37 points, three more

*Remembering the 1960 final. (from left) Norman Deeley,
Ronnie Clayton, Peter Broadbent and Stan Cullis.*

*The cover of the programme. The 1 shilling price is worth 5p today!
Courtesy Wolverhampton Wanderers*

Bill Slater and Ronnie Clayton shake hands before the kick-off, watched by referee Kevin Howley.

Matt Woods tackles Jimmy Murray.
Offside Photography.

Malcolm Finalyson swings on the cross bar as Gerry Harris watches.
Offside Photography.

Malcolm Finlayson dives at the feet of Bryan Douglas ...

*... and needs attention. Bill Slater, referee Kevin
Howley, and George Showell (standing), and Gerry Harris (kneeling)
watch as he is treated by. trainer Joe Gardiner Offside Photography.*

Norman Deeley follows Mick McGrath's own goal into the net. Dave Whelan can only watch.

Matt Woods rises high to head clear.
Offside Photography.

Harry Leyland stretches to divert the ball away from Barry Stobart and Peter Broadbent (10) Offside Photography.

Bill Slater is hoisted aloft by Ron Flowers and Peter Broadbent. Standing (from left) are Gerry Harris, Malcolm Finlayson, Eddie Clamp and George Showell. In front are Barry Stobart, Des Horne and Jimmy Murray. Courtesy Wolverhampton Wanderers

Eddie Clamp and Bill Slater run with the cup while Norman Deeley follows. Courtesy Wolverhampton Wanderers

Blackburn captain Ronnie Clayton visits the Wolves dressing room to congratulate George Showell. Des Horne is on the bench. Offside Photography.

Peter Broadbent, Gerry Mannion and Malcolm Finlayson show off the cup. Courtesy Wolverhampton Wanderers

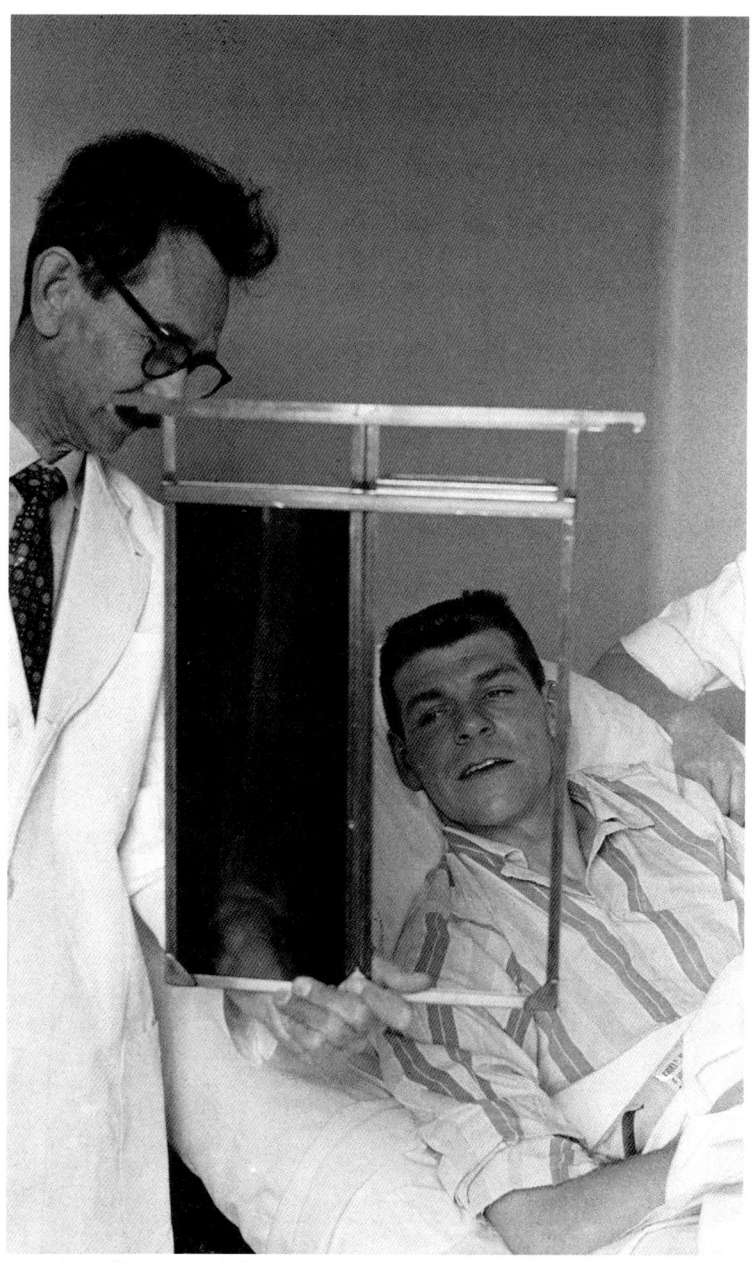

While all Dave Whelan has to look at is an X-ray of his broken leg.
Offside Photography.

Wolves bring back the cup to fans cramming the streets of Wolverhampton.

than Leeds in 21st and seven more than Luton Town at the bottom. The east Lancashire side marched off to Wembley in poor form.

Wolves' final league game of the season was at Stamford Bridge. Before the game Burnley knew that if they got three points (a win and a draw in those days) from their games with Fulham at Turf Moor and Manchester City at Maine Road that the title would be theirs. All Wolves could do was win at Chelsea and hope for the best. Spurs needed to beat Blackpool at White Hart Lane (which they did 4-1) and hope that Wolves and Burnley failed to get any more points.

The table read:

Wolves	41	101-66	52
Burnley	40	83-60	52
Spurs	41	82-49	51

Cullis, angered by the poor display against Spurs, made changes for Stamford Bridge – out went Bobby Mason and Gerry Mannion, struggling after his impressive start, and back came Des Horne at outside-left with Norman Deeley switching across to his preferred right-wing position, and Barry Stobart at inside right. This was his first appearance as an inside forward and it was to have major repercussions when the team for the FA Cup final was chosen.

It was a resurgent Wolves who, despite falling behind to a Ron Tindall goal, swept away Chelsea to win 5-1. Horne had a fine match, scoring two great goals and making a third after a brilliant run. Murray, Flowers and Broadbent were the other scorers as 61,657 spectators applauded Wolves off the pitch at the end.

Writing in the following day's *Sunday People*, Maurice Smith gave an early indication of the heartbreak that was to follow later in the week for Bobby Mason: "My reading of the Cullis intention is that this line-up which made Chelsea look like a Second Division defence will be on duty for the last round-up next Saturday."

When the news from Turf Moor came through that Burnley had drawn 0-0 with Fulham, Wolves knew the title would again be theirs if the east Lancashire side failed to win at Maine Road in their final match on the Monday.

Meanwhile, Tom Finney ended his fabulous career as Preston North End beat relegated Luton Town 2-0 at home. Finney ran off having made 473 first team appearances for his hometown and only club for which, despite playing the majority of games on the wing, he scored 210 goals. During his time at Deepdale Preston finished second in the league in 1952–53 and 1957–58, and as FA Cup runners-up in 1954.

Bill Slater is a big fan of Tom Finney: "If you were picking a team and your life depended on it you'd pick Tom Finney. I'd play him at centre-forward but he was also a great winger. He is in my top five English players that I played against, along with Bert Williams in goal, Billy Wright at centre-half, Duncan

Leading up to the Final

Edwards in midfield and Bobby Charlton just slightly further forward."

With Stan Cullis sitting in the Maine Road directors' box close to Harry Potts' wife Margaret – "He had a face like a stone,' she said – the match proved a nervous affair. But Trevor Meredith, stand-in for the injured outside-right John Connelly, scored the winner to give Burnley their first title since 1920–21. All Cullis could do was offer his congratulations to Potts, a one-time Wolves coach, and look forward to Wembley.

Bill Slater recalls: "I certainly wasn't devastated when we heard the result from Maine Road. I felt we'd lost the league title when we played so badly against Tottenham Hotspur. Burnley had a fine side, in which Jimmy McIlroy was outstanding, although on our day I felt we could beat them, as we had showed only a few weeks earlier.

"But the table after 42 matches doesn't lie. I had the pleasure of winning two league titles so you can't grumble; and anyway, we had Wembley to look forward to."

On the Thursday Slater had the pleasure of hearing he'd been voted the Football Writers' Footballer of the Year, pipping McIlroy for the prestigious award. Slater became the second Wolves player to be voted number one, as Billy Wright had won the award at the end of the 1951–52 season.

"It was great to get it, but I saw it and still do as an award for the team and our efforts that season in which we came close to doing the double. I was lucky as I was the captain of the side when the votes were counted," says Slater modestly.

Slater had, of course, taken over as captain from Eddie Stuart not too long before but he was to retain the job over the next few seasons and in his autobiography, *For Wolves and England*, Ron Flowers thought highly enough of him to write that: "With his polish, ability to speak fluently, and tremendous zest for football, Bill Slater has emerged as an outstanding skipper. In addition Bill is a player who fights from the beginning to the end of every match. No game is lost until it is won, is the attitude Bill takes, and he spreads it through the team he skippers. Whilst off the field he has revealed himself as an outstanding scholar, he has also proved on it that he possesses the ability to lead men. And to win their respect."

As we know, reaching the Cup final was the zenith for players but the 23rd man on the pitch was equally thrilled to be there. And the man chosen to referee the final in 1960 was Kevin Howley from Billingham, County Durham, at 35 the youngest man to take charge of an FA Cup final. His linesmen were R.H. Windle and F. Reid of Derbyshire and Hertfordshire.

The Week before Wembley

FOLLOWING THE final league fixtures the previous Saturday the teams had a week to prepare for the big day. For Blackburn it was a second Wembley appearance; while Wolves had been there twice before.

Having beaten Blackburn home and away in the League and only just lost out to Burnley for the title, Wolves were overwhelming favourites. But their older fans could recall that they'd also been strongly fancied before the 1939 FA Cup final, only to lose 4-1 to Portsmouth.

Rovers' older fans remembered that the previous time their side had made it to Wembley, in 1928, they had run out as massive underdogs to Huddersfield Town, League winners in three consecutive seasons between 1924 and 1926 and runners-up in the next two seasons. Yet Rovers, with two goals from Jack Roscamp, one within the first sixty seconds, and one from Tommy McLean, proved enough to ensure that Alec Jackson's goal was only a consolation for the Yorkshire side.

Rovers, therefore, were not without hope and their players were confident of capturing the trophy for the seventh time in the club's long history. But they also knew that most of their victories had come in the Cup's early years. If they had to go back 32 years

Fifty Years On

for their previous success, the one before that was in 1890–91. But after losing to Old Etonians in their first final in 1881-82 they had won three years in a row from 1884. There were three barren years before they won it again in 1889–90 and the following year.

Since that first defeat, Blackburn had won every time they reached the final, so, Rovers fans argued, history was on their side. To reinforce that feeling, Jock Crawford, the 1928 Rovers keeper, was on hand to pass on a lucky pin to Harry Leyland. It had been given to him by Herby Arthur, his counterpart in the team which had won the cup three years in a row. He had got it from a Blackburn businessman prior to the 1884 final – would it now be a case of seventh time lucky?

Wolves, of course, had their own FA Cup pedigree and were bidding for their fourth victory. They had beaten Everton 1-0 in 1893, Newcastle United 3-1 in 1908 and Leicester City 3-1 in 1949.

The finalists had been drawn against each other seven times in the FA Cup with Blackburn having the edge, four-three. The last time was 40 years before when Wolves won a first round replay at Ewood Park with a goal from Tancy Lea.

Much of the media interest in cup final week centred on whether Wolves manager Stan Cullis would keep the team which had played so superbly at Stamford Bridge. The alternative was to restore Bobby Mason, who had played in every round so far, in place of Barry Stobart. If Stobart played, only Charlton's Arthur Turner would have made an appearance in

The Week before Wembley

a final after so few appearances. Turner had played in nine of Charlton's ten FA Cup matches in 1945–46 (the FA Cup was played on a home and away basis that year) but never made a league appearance for Charlton. Stobart, whose usual position was centre-forward, had made just four league and one FA Cup appearance for Wolves.

If Mason was to be left out there would not even be the consolation of sitting on the bench hoping to get on, as substitutes were not allowed in the final until 1967.

Mason must have feared the worst. After all, in 1949 the regular full-back Lol Kelly, who, after being injured in the first match, had missed the FA Cup semi-final replay victory over Matt Busby's Manchester United and the league games that followed, was left out of the Wolves Cup final side despite recovering in time. Stan Cullis had been the manager.

According to Billy Wright, when Kelly found out he wasn't in the side "he got off the coach at Oxford as the team travelled south on the Thursday before the final. He was that upset and disappointed; it absolutely broke his heart. Stan threatened him with all sorts of consequences but the matter was never mentioned again. I think the manager put himself in Lol's shoes when he had calmed down and realised how he would have reacted."

Yet on the Tuesday of cup week Bobby Mason's hopes must have soared when he was handed the number eight shirt to wear for the souvenir programme. It was not to be and two days later his heart was broken when Cullis took him to one side and explained he would be selecting the inexperienced Stobart in his place. Later the manager told the press that he knew "how disappointing it must be to be left out, but he has just got to accept it". Yet he admitted he didn't know "just how Mason has taken it. After all, how do you know what is in a man's mind?"

Bob Pennington, in the *Daily Express*, said he understood that Mason was disappointed. This must be viewed as a massive understatement. Fifty years later when researching this book I received a letter from Bobby Mason responding to my request for an interview with the simple but terse reply stating in bold type: "Sorry but I will not take part in your cup final campaign."

Malcolm Finlayson says: "I didn't think Bobby would be interviewed. He was ever so upset; he had played in a lot of big games, Bobby, and he was a cracking player. But the FA Cup final was an extra-special event. To miss it was a big blow. I believe that he was offered a medal as one of the players who had played during the tournament but refused to accept it."

Bobby Mason was indeed a "cracking player". During his career at Molineux he won two league winner's medals and made 173 first team appearances in which he notched a highly impressive 54 goals. Ironically, 1959–60 had been his best season in terms of goals. He scored 15 times. Locally born – in Tipton – his non-stop commitment and ability to bring other forwards into play made him a firm favourite with the Molineux faithful. He played for Wolves for another two years but with modest success before moving to Chelmsford, Leyton Orient and Poole Town.

Eddie Stuart was the other Wolves regular to miss the final, having found his way back blocked by the impressive performances of George Showell. But he had been out since late February and, unlike Mason, was aware he was unlikely to play at Wembley.

Stuart had started the season as captain: "I just couldn't put into words my disappointment at not playing at Wembley; it was the most devastating moment in my life. I have mixed feelings about the 1959–60 season. At the start I was made captain to replace the great Billy Wright. It was one of the proudest moments of my life. I would have become the first South African ever to have captained the winners of the FA Cup. I was the 12th man at Wembley, but of course I knew I wouldn't get on."

In a fine career Stuart made 322 first team appearances and was outstanding in the last dozen matches of Wolves' 1953–54 championship-winning season. After winning championship medals in 1958 and 1959, and collecting an FA Cup winner's medal as reserve at Wembley, he moved to Stoke City in the summer of 1962 where, along with Stanley Matthews and several veteran stars signed by manager Tony Waddington, including Burnley's Jimmy McIlroy, he helped inspire the Potters to the Division Two title.

Meanwhile, in the Rovers camp, manager Dally Duncan's concerns were focused on whether their charismatic centre-forward Derek Dougan would be fit. His loss would be a big blow as Rovers were banking on the Northern Ireland international being able to use his pace to unsettle Bill Slater. This point was made by Bob Pennington on the morning of the final when he backed Rovers to win as "Dougan is deceptively fast – Wolves' centre-half is suspect in his speed of recovery. That could be fatal for Wolves if Dougan's thigh injury allows him to go flat out."

In fact Dougan's injury was never going to do that. He should not have played because his lack of full fitness gave Rovers an additional burden to carry.

Matt Woods takes up the story: "Dougan had pulled a muscle a week previously. It was up to him to decide whether he was fit. In those days the Cup final, and playing in it, meant everything. He must have thought he could get through the match. So Dougan took his once-in-a-lifetime opportunity and played – and after about ten minutes it was obvious he was only half fit."

His half-back colleague Mick McGrath is less sympathetic to 'The Doog' and is also critical of manager Duncan, saying: "We knew he was injured but you leave it up to the honesty of the player. You ask the player, and Doog said he was fine but after ten minutes it was obvious he was going to be a waste of space that day.

"Our previous manager, Johnny Carey, had said that Duncan was too nice a guy and I partly feel he was right. Sometimes as a manager you have to be hard and cruel because there were so many different temperaments to deal with and I think this is what happened with Dougan. I certainly think he should have put him under more pressure to think about whether he was 100 per cent fit.

"In the manager's defence, the two players looking to play in Derek's position, Eddie Thomas and Roy Isherwood, hadn't had a lot of matches."

That might well be true but Isherwood, at least, had shown impressive form in the vital victory over Leeds which ensured Rovers' First Division safety and had travelled south with the Blackburn squad along with Thomas, who was selected as 12th man. Also in the party was an up-and-coming star, Mike England, who seven years later would be part of the Spurs FA Cup winning team.

Perhaps if Isherwood had been a straight swap it might have made it easier for Duncan to have left out Dougan, but he was a winger and had he been selected the attack would have needed reshuffling. It is, however, interesting to note that in December 1960, when Jack Marshall, who had taken over from Duncan as the Rovers manager, dropped Dougan and brought in Isherwood, the move of Ally MacLeod to centre-forward helped produce one of Rovers' finest performances that year, a 5-1 Ewood Park demolition of Fulham.

Writing years after the event, Dougan admitted he wasn't fit, saying that "vanity triumphed over common sense. On Wednesday the chairman was quoted in the Press demanding to know whether I was fit. This made me angry. They seemed to be forcing a decision. At the ground I was told to prove that I was fit for Saturday. Gritting my teeth, like they do in war films when told 'This is it, men!', I put my leg to the test. The pain made me wince, but I took care no one noticed. They were not watching my face; they were watching how I ran. If I could put on a good show to convince them I was all right I would have the rest of the week to recover. After a few laps around the track it was agreed to have the final fitness test on the morning of the match.

"The rest of the week was spent in agony, mental and physical. Should I admit I was not fit or force myself to play? On Friday, without extending myself, I was able to sprint at the pace of some of the other players... and after a five-a-side game I declared myself fit. Perhaps I thought the team could carry me as we had played well in the previous rounds. It was my first Cup Final and I took a chance. My heart ruled my head."

Blackburn also had concerns that Harry Leyland would miss the big day and reserve keeper Bob Jones travelled to London, staying with relatives in Fulham and no doubt hoping to get a game. Leyland, though, was fit and Jones missed out.

Bryan Douglas had an eventful pre-match morning. He says: "On the Friday night I came back with the team from a cinema visit to receive a telegram saying 'congratulations' and telling me that my son, who wasn't expected until the end of June, had been born and that my wife and baby were at University College hospital in London.

The Week before Wembley

"I was desperate to see them and so the following morning I asked the manager if I could go. He said yes, but to make sure I was back at 12.30pm, as the bus for Wembley would leave then. I had to get a bus to Golders Green tube, then a tube to Euston and then I walked up to the hospital which was about 15 minutes away. I saw them – my wife and Graham – for 15 minutes before doing the return journey and getting back to the hotel for 12.15pm. I paid my own fare there and back. I have no idea whether I'd have played if I missed the bus, mind."

The fans of both clubs were also pouring into Euston by train before taking the tube to Wembley or driving, in those days mostly by coach, to north-west London. Steve Gordos sums up the feeling: "When I was a young lad the FA Cup was *the* thing. The FA Cup final was the only match to be shown live in its entirety on TV at the time and I would have loved to have watched my team on television but you had to be at Wembley to see Wolves. It was what you dreamed about as a boy. It was great to walk up Wembley Way to be supporting Wolverhampton Wanderers. It was magic to see the Twin Towers. My team at Wembley – brilliant. The magic has gone out of the FA Cup today, but not then."

Rovers fan William Jeffries, now 58, recalls: "We stood up at Wembley – I seem to recall the match tickets were 3s 6d (18p). My dad was made up we were going to Wembley; some of my friends who couldn't get tickets were a wee bit jealous. I had to recount my experiences at school on the Monday. My mam, who was coming up to 40 years old, had never been to London before. Neither, of course, had I. We made up giant rosettes, people had big wooden rattles – we packed the bag, sandwiches, flask of coffee and a drop of rum for my dad, to which he was a bit partial.

"We left late on the Friday night and as we walked up to the station there were thousands around and everyone seemed to be in blue and white. My dad took me up to the engine at the front. There was a carnival atmosphere.

"There were six of us in the compartment. I managed to get some sleep but not much, as it was like going to the moon. When we arrived there was a tour round London after we had our breakfast and we saw all the sights. We came back at midnight but there certainly weren't as many people around when we got back as when we left – the streets were eerily quiet."

Another Rovers fan, Kenneth Roberts, now 80, recalls: "There was loads of banter with the Wolves fans going up Wembley Way; people had rattles and trumpets, and many wore giant rosettes. It was great to be going to Wembley to see your side in the FA Cup final but there was concern when we heard that Dougan had apparently asked for a transfer. No one could really believe it was true."

But it was – Dougan had chosen to post a transfer request on the morning of the club's most important match for more than three decades. Perhaps more importantly, news of this had leaked out. Whether this was through Dougan speaking to the press or someone else he'd told we shall probably never know as the man himself died in June 2007.

The players, too, had to come to terms with Dougan's bombshell. Bryan Douglas says: "He was a good footballer who could have been better. He liked himself better than the game, but he was bloody fast, long and lanky and got vital goals.

"One of his relatives upset some of us when he died a few years back by saying that the other players had let him down and that's why he handed in a transfer request before the cup final. They said it was because the extra money we'd agreed with the club for getting to the final hadn't been paid. The fact was that, under the rules in place, the club wasn't allowed to pay us any extra money.

"The FA paid the winners £1,100 and the losers £880. This was £100 per position for the winners. Each player got a cut based on the number of games you'd played of the £100 or £80 you got for the losers. I was forced to defend the other players in a recent Rovers programme but, typical Derek, even in death there was some controversy.

"That aside we were badly paid in those days. When the maximum wage ended we were all on £20 a week. As a youngster I lived just 500 yards from the Rovers ground and so when they asked me to sign as a schoolboy I was really pleased, but over the next few years another eight or nine clubs approached me, including Bolton, Blackpool, Arsenal and Wolverhampton.

"But as there was no money to be gained by going elsewhere, due to the rules that restricted what clubs could pay players, then there would have been no point in moving anyway. I was simply flattered by their interest and kept on playing and making progress with Rovers.

"My dad made sure, however, that when I left school I got an apprenticeship as a motor mechanic as football was, and still is, a precarious way of earning a living and an injury can finish you.

"However, I was having to take that much time off that eventually the firm said I had to make a choice and Jackie Bestall wanted me to go on the ground staff at Blackburn so I started out earning £6 a week, which was good money. I was aged 17. Ronnie Clayton started out at the same time, but at 18 I had to go on National Service. I didn't like the idea as I felt that it was going to take two years out of what would be a short career – in fact I actually enjoyed the two years and met some really good people during that time.

"I made my debut whilst I was in the services, but when I left I got married and then in 1954 I got back into the side and things went well for me, and they really took off in the second season when I managed to grab 15 goals and also get into the England B side. I then went on an under-23 tour alongside well-known players such as Ronnie Clayton, Bobby Charlton and Duncan Edwards – all terrific players and people.

"I think what helped me was the fact that I had done well in games in London, which meant the pressmen who saw me wrote good things. Also the man who oversaw the team, Walter Winterbottom, was keen on seeing a player away from home. As records show, most teams do better at home so it was a chance to judge a player and his character in circumstances unfamiliar to the player.

"Despite the relatively poor wages we received – compared to today they were *very* poor – I still loved, and I stress loved, being a professional footballer. It was like being in a pantomime. It was sheer joy and we played a game that millions would have given their right arm to play. My friends were envious, and also I played in a good side with Rovers.

"What I think held us back was that we had no squad of players. I know that most clubs then had a core of players, but ours was very small and I feel that whilst we had some very good players up front that we lacked cover at the back."

Mick McGrath also knew that Dougan wanted to move. "I was aware of that well before we got to Wembley as myself and John Bray shared a room and we were breakfasting in bed and talking about it – it was a bombshell. But no one argued with him as everyone was concentrating and looking forward to the biggest single day of our footballing careers. There was a good atmosphere amongst the players which I don't think anyone wanted to ruin."

According to Dougan, writing years later, he had made six previous verbal requests for a transfer and all had been refused. He had found Blackburn a drab, depressing place and claimed that a player knows his time is always running out in football.

He also claimed that the training at Blackburn was "a joke", consisting of a couple of laps around the ground, that the club didn't have a training ground and regularly used a small patch of ground called "Little Wembley" that doubled as a car park on match days. Far too much, he felt, was left to the players' instinct.

This may well be true – but to damage team morale by putting in a transfer request before the FA Cup final is astonishing. Couldn't it have waited? Was it not a case of publicity seeking? Not according to Dougan, who claimed he was only conscious of wanting to leave Blackburn and had already flown to Belgium to discuss terms with a club. He hoped to show that by placing a transfer request at a time when he should have been at his happiest he really was determined to move on.

Later Dougan did express regret for his action, writing: "I realise now, with hindsight, that my timing was unfortunate and my request in the circumstances was an insult to the club on its way to Wembley. If I live to be 100 I shall always regret my action, but any young man in whatever walk of life needs the right environment to inspire him and I did not have this at Blackburn."

Ironically, Dougan received a high-profile letter himself just days beforehand when he was sent a "Good Luck" message by Clint Walker, star of the American TV series *Cheyenne*. That was Dougan's nickname at the time due to his resemblance to the actor.

Steve Gordos, Bill Jeffries and Kenneth Roberts were among the lucky ones because, as thousands then and since have found, Cup final tickets are hard to come by. Today clubs can expect to share around 45,000 tickets, roughly half the capacity of a redesigned Wembley. In 1960 it was just 30,000 of the 100,000 tickets, up from just 25,000 in 1955.

This distribution system was wide open to abuse as some 40,000 tickets were given to the FA's county associations, who distributed them to minor clubs. These were supposed to be a reward for keeping football going at the grass roots, but in reality many ended up on the black market, sold by spivs for vastly inflated rates to fans desperate to see their side on the big day.

Of course, 30,000 to the finalists plus 40,000 to the counties still makes only 70,000. So where did the other 30,000 go? The Sunderland legend Len Shackleton, whose appearances for England were restricted due to his unwillingness to defer to the selectors. had no doubt, saying in his book *The Clown Prince of Soccer*, published in the 1950s: "Unfortunately the Cup final is no longer treated as a football match: it is a social occasion with all the trimmings – soccer's answer to Ascot, Wimbledon and Lord's – and as befits such a gala day, must be attended by everyone who is anyone in society's circles."

Shackleton had played in the Young v Old England game at Highbury the night before the 1954 final, a traditional curtain-raiser, and asked an FA official for a ticket for the final only to be refused. He telephoned a friend in the fishery business who sorted out two for him and his wife.

The low level of wages had meant that players were not averse to the idea of earning a few pounds themselves by selling tickets and by 1960 they were officially restricted to just twelve each. This was as a result of a court case in 1952 when Newcastle captain Joe Harvey was found to have been selling his tickets.

For fans unable to watch the game live there was black and white TV, and coverage of the final dominated the weekend. In 1960, and for many years following, the FA Cup final was a national cultural and social event that was discussed for weeks before and after. The whole day would be taken up watching hours of pre-match TV entertainment, then the game itself, the presentation of the FA Cup and reading about it in the following day's newspapers.

The 1937 final between Preston North End and Sunderland was the first to attract TV cameras but the first final to be televised live in its entirety was a year later when Preston beat Huddersfield 1-0 with George Mutch's penalty decider coming in the last minute of extra time. The TV audience was estimated at just 10,000.

The Final

BRYAN DOUGLAS rated Wolves highly: "They were a very solid side. At full back they had Showell and Harris. Harris was just one of those players I could never master. He seemed to know what I was going to do, and the halfback line with Ron Flowers, Bill Slater and Eddie Clamp was extremely good. I knew we would have to play very well to beat them."

The teams lined up, on paper, in the traditional 2-3-5 formation of two full backs, three half backs and five forwards. However, on the field itself the formation was the typical W-M formation originally developed by the great Huddersfield and Arsenal manager Herbert Chapman of the 1920s and 1930s, which meant the centre-half dropped back between the full-backs and one of the two wing-halves was essentially a defensive player.

The other wing-half joined one of the inside forwards as the engine room in midfield while the other inside forward had mainly attacking duties, often joining the two wingers and the centre-forward in attack.

The teams were:
Wolves: Finlayson; Showell, Harris; Clamp, Slater, Flowers; Deeley, Stobart, Murray, Broadbent, Horne.
Blackburn: Leyland; Bray, Whelan; Clayton, Woods,

McGrath; Bimpson, Dobing, Dougan, Douglas, MacLeod.

The selection of John Bray at full back saw him follow in the footsteps of his uncles Jack and George, who had played in FA Cup finals for Manchester City (1933 and 1934) and Burnley (1947) respectively.

The match gets under way

The 100,000 crowd baked in sunshine with temperatures well into the 90s. It was going to be a difficult afternoon.

And it was to become much more difficult for Rovers after just five minutes. Bryan Douglas explains: "I got away up the middle and had to decide whether to take Slater on but I decided to hold the ball and then I slipped it through to Dougan in the left-hand position. Now if he'd been fully fit he would have been on to it like a rabbit, but it virtually rolled out of play.

"I am still bloody angry at him even now. I think Stan Cullis would have been a bit more rigorous in finding out whether Dougan had been fully fit if he'd been in the Wolves side. We were set to play one of the best sides in the country on a sweltering hot day with only ten fit men. With eleven players it would have been difficult enough but with ten it was going to be almost impossible."

The Final

Bill Slater says he had no idea Dougan was not fully fit. He also questions whether it would have made any difference if the maverick striker had not been carrying an injury. "It was only later that I found out that some reporters had suggested Dougan's pace might be a key factor in turning the Cup final Blackburn's way and that he was going to be able to beat me for pace.

"I wasn't particularly slow and I'd also like to think I could anticipate where the ball might get played as well. I certainly had no intention of not playing my usual game. I had played against Derek previously and done well against him, so had nothing particularly to fear.

"I recall that years later Derek Dougan was a guest speaker at an event I attended, and he mentioned that I was in the audience and he said he always enjoyed playing against me, as I couldn't run as fast as him. That was fine by me. But I did ask him how many games he had played against me and how many goals he had scored. He didn't know so I was happy to tell him the answers were eight and none. It brought a big laugh but I am not sure he was that pleased."

Steve Gordos confirms Slater's opinion: "Bill Slater had the knack of always being in the right place at the right time. Years later you saw that same ability in Bobby Moore and Paul McGrath. It's not about being fleet of foot, it's about having a fast football brain. Slater had one and that meant he could read the game."

Fifty Years On

Despite Dougan's lack of mobility, it was still Rovers who fashioned the first real scoring opportunity when Bimpson's shot from Dobing's pass forced Finlayson to tip the ball over the bar.

The match became something of a midfield slog after that and with neither side displaying any great fluency, there was little to trouble either keeper, although Leyland had to be alert when Broadbent threatened to head home a cross from Clamp on the byline.

With seven minutes left to half-time Horne might have given Wolves the lead when he cut in to fire a cross shot that Leyland did well to touch round the post. His opposite number had to be equally alert a minute later after Dobing's tenacious run through the middle. But Finlayson, showing great alertness, was out swiftly to block Dobing's shot with his legs.

Matt Woods remembers: "Peter Dobing was clean through and with his skill I thought he'd open the scoring but he smashed his shot against Finlayson's legs and the chance was lost."

Mick McGrath says: "I think it was Wembley that got to Peter. I just think he froze. On another day he would have tucked that chance away to give us the lead."

The Scotsman's save became even more important when, within less than a minute, Wolves opened the scoring with a fortunate goal. McGrath says that before the match Dally Duncan had told his team that Wolves, with two wingers, would drive the ball hard and low across the goals, making it difficult for defenders. It was this tactic that had brought the Black Country side two points back at Ewood Park in January, when Matt Woods had inadvertently knocked Des Horne's cross past Harry Leyland in the last few minutes for the only goal of the game.

This time the goal came with four minutes of the first period remaining. Ron Flowers burst through to find Stobart on the Wolves left. With Norman Deeley screaming for the ball, the youngster cut inside to drive a low cross. Sadly for Mick McGrath, in his efforts to clear the ball, he succeeded only in squeezing it past Leyland, who had advanced from his line to cut out the cross.

McGrath, painfully, remembers the goal only too well. "Stobart hit this ball hard and low across the face of the goal and I tried to get outside the near post to knock it for a corner, but Harry's coming out behind me and it hit my toe and flew off into the back of the net. I felt the ground was going to open up and swallow me. At half-time Harry said, 'Did you not hear me bloody shout?' I didn't."

Matt Woods says: "It was just one of those things. If he'd left it either I or Harry would have dealt with it. We'd gone from having a chance to be one up to being one down in a matter of a minute."

Deeley offered a different option, claiming that had McGrath missed the ball he would have forced it home anyway. There were many in the ground under the misapprehension that the Wolves winger had, in fact, scored because in following the ball into the net he was left hanging from the rigging in celebration.

It was only the second own goal in a Wembley FA Cup final. The first was scored by Bert Turner when Charlton Athletic side were beaten 4-1 by Derby County in 1946. But Turner had the consolation of also scoring at the other end.

McGrath says that, despite his mistake, "Nobody blamed me as in all honesty we never had a chance of winning."

The reason for such pessimism was that in the 43rd minute Blackburn were undone catastrophically. Left-back Dave Whelan was stretchered off with a broken leg.

According to Alan Hoby's report in the *Sunday Express*, the tragedy happened "when the tormenting hard-dribbling Norman Deeley clashed and collided with Blackburn's left-back Dave Whelan. They struck shins, Deeley spun away like a black and gold top – but amid a strained silence Whelan lay motionless, a sad prostrate blue and white figure.

"For two minutes Whelan lay ominously still while the St John Ambulance men and stretcher-bearers fussed about him. Then tenderly they tied his feet together and laid him with delicate care on the stretcher. Dave Whelan had fractured his right shin." Hoby got it wrong. Whelan had broken his left leg.

Dave Whelan remains angry at what he feels was a bad tackle by Deeley. Forty-five years later, several newspapers quoted him after a reckless challenge by Chelsea's Michael Essien on Liverpool's Dietmar Hamann during a European Champions League game in December 2005: "The worst tackle I've seen

The Final

for a long time. You can't go over the top like that. It was so dangerous. It has no place in football. How Hamann didn't break his leg, I'll never know.

"Essien's tackle was like the one that broke my leg in the Cup Final in 1960. Norman Deeley went over the top, but it was different then, there were no TV replays. The referee didn't even give a foul, but it absolutely finished me. It was a nasty tackle."

Writing in *Dave Whelan: Playing to Win* in 2009, the Wigan chairman, who went on to build a successful business empire after retiring from playing, admits he was intent on intimidating Deeley from the off, and: "After about twenty minutes I got him in a tackle and I really hurt him. He was getting away from me, so I just clogged him, perhaps a little unfairly but not by the standards of the day. 'He's finished for the rest of the game, he won't bother me now,' I thought.

"In the 42nd minute a 50-50 ball came in between me and Norman Deeley. I thought he would still be trying to get there ahead of me, even after the crunch I'd just given him. He was that type of player. So I set off, determined to win the ball.

"And I did. I got there seconds before Deeley. But that was when I realised he had no intention at all of racing me for that ball. He was going for me. As I was running I heard a loud crack and felt my knee suddenly burn with pain… I was in agony and I knew I was out of the game. Norman Deeley had got me."

Dave Whelan's career at the top level had come to an end, because while he was still able to play professionally it was in the Fourth Division at Crewe. He never played for the Rovers first team again and moved to Gresty Road in January 1963. His problems might have been even worse as only the swift intervention of a hospital doctor in advising him to have the plaster removed stopped the spread of gangrene.Dave Whelan is correct that today the incident would be replayed numerous times on television. This wasn't the case in 1960 – there were just four BBC cameras covering the match – and it was not until many years later that a DVD of the game was released. This shows Whelan taking out Deeley early in the match, but when it comes to showing the incident in which his leg was broken it appears to show no more than two keenly committed players going honestly for the ball, with, if anything, Whelan slightly late. It was Deeley who got to the ball first. Whelan's view, not surprisingly, has brought a response from players and fans on both sides.

After Whelan's comments in 2005, Steve Gordos wrote to him. "I don't recall any blame being attached to Deeley. Whelan even appears to wave to Deeley as he is stretchered off to say it was 'no problem'.

"I've replayed a DVD of the game, which shows clearly that Deeley got to the ball first while Whelan comes careering in with his left leg at an awkward angle. Deeley could not avoid tripping over the leg. I believe if Mr Whelan viewed the incident again, he would see that his memory is wrong. He has done a great disservice to Norman Deeley, who always played fairly."

The Final

Gordos asked Whelan to retract his comments on Deeley but did not receive a reply.

Gordos is also angry at Whelan for the comments in his autobiography. "I was incensed by Whelan's comments suggesting that Norman made a two-footed tackle on Whelan. He compared it to a bad tackle by Essien of Chelsea, which was ridiculous. I wrote to Whelan about this and called on him to watch the DVD of the game and then he would surely apologise. I also wrote to the *Daily Mail*, who had carried the article quoting Whelan, and they published my letter asking him to take a look at the DVD that is now available.

"Whelan never had the decency to write back, which seems most out of character as he always comes across as a fair-minded fellow. What he said was most unfair to Norman Deeley, who was one the game's gentlemen. If you look at the incident it's clear that Whelan's version is totally wrong. Repeating his comments four years later is out of order."

Deeley's old teammates are also concerned. Malcolm Finlayson says: "I am a bit upset, to be honest, because at the time, and afterwards, Ronnie Clayton, a very sporting man who shook our hands afterwards as we waited to go and collect our medals, acknowledged it was an accident."

Bill Slater says: "I seem to remember the referee didn't even award a free kick against Norman Deeley, who was a tiny chap. I am aware that Whelan has suggested recently he was deliberately fouled but

I thought he just sort of fell over with both players going honestly for the ball."

George Showell says: "I was at school with Norman Deeley and any idea he did anything to harm Dave Whelan deliberately is nonsense."

Whelan's teammate Bryan Douglas meanwhile admits he's "not sure about Dave's injury. I just think he went with his wrong leg. He was a right-footer but played on the left. I have heard that Dave thought he'd gone over the top but I met Norman Deeley later and I think he's a genuine guy."

Deeley, who died in 2007, had this to say on the incident many years later in an article in the book *Match of My Life: Wolves*: "The ball was knocked out towards me as I ran inside off the wing. It was a bit short and so tempted Dave Whelan into the tackle. I might only be short, but I could tackle as well as any Wolves player, because I'd started out as a half back. Dave and I went for this ball and we arrived at speed pretty much together. Crunch. I heard this crack as we collided and I thought 'That's my leg.' When I looked down in my dazed state there was a duck-egg shaped bump already forming on my shins. Then I looked across at Dave's leg and there was no flesh on it for about four or five inches… I had a few questions afterwards about the incident by the press but generally it was accepted as an accident."

While writing this book I made attempts to interview Dave Whelan and only bad weather prevented the first meeting. When it later became

The Final

increasingly difficult to contact him I wrote asking for an interview but never received a reply.

Whelan's broken leg meant that for the seventh time in nine seasons a player had suffered a serious injury playing in the FA Cup final. It is perhaps not surprising that in only two cases did the suffering team go on to win.

It was a devastating blow to Blackburn. Bryan Douglas remembers: "When Dave Whelan broke his leg that left us with just nine players. True, Dougan was on the field, but he may as well not have been. We were playing a very good side with one arm tied behind out backs."

Rovers attempted to overcome the handicap as the second half opened. They pushed back eleven-man Wolves having reshuffled their line-up. McGrath dropped to left-back leaving Ally MacLeod to rove between left half and the left wing. He was to do a magnificent job, ending up winning the Man of the Match award.

Bryan Douglas says: "Ally had a good game at Wembley. He was a useful player and got some vital goals. He was a good friend of mine and was certainly a character. He talked a very good game and proved himself to be a first-rate salesman when he got the Scots convinced they were going to win the World Cup in Argentina in 1978."

But despite this promising period the match was as good as settled on 67 minutes. Des Horne crossed from the byline for Deeley, who had limped back out at the restart, to sweep the ball into the net. Rovers defenders protested strongly that he was offside, claiming that Mick McGrath standing behind the goal line in the net was out of play and as such Horne was offside when he crossed the ball.

Matt Woods is still aggrieved. "I still feel the second goal was a mile offside. We used to get out quick and play offside; we all came out together. Mick McGrath was in the goal behind the line but had his hand on the post and when Deeley knocked it home the referee said that Mick was playing him on. He wasn't and that killed us. We appealed but it had no effect."

After the game referee Howley justified his decision to award the goal by saying he thought McGrath's action was "an act of gamesmanship. That was why I allowed the goal."

Shortly afterwards Flowers thought he'd made it 3-0 when he hit the ball into the net from an Eddie Clamp cross, only to be ruled offside. But just before the final whistle Deeley grabbed his second when Leyland was helpless to prevent Stobart's centre rebounding off the post and giving the tiny winger a chance he eagerly accepted. Some in the crowd thought it was his hat-trick.

Getting a winner's medal was particularly exciting for George Showell, who had missed out on league winner's medals because he had not played the minimum qualifying number of games in the 1957–58 and 1958–59 league seasons.

"When I was left out before the Newcastle United game in the third round I was devastated. When

The Final

Billy Wright retired it was my chance to establish myself and so to be dropped to twelfth man was heartbreaking. But I was determined not to go down without fighting, and I resolved to work hard in training and ensure that when I got my chance in the first team I played as well as I could and stayed in the team. It meant that I picked up a priceless FA Cup winner's medal, something that I still treasure."

As the Wolves team followed their captain Bill Slater up the 39 Wembley steps to the Royal Box to receive the trophy from the Duchess of Gloucester, many of the crowd were so disappointed by what they'd witnessed that they booed. This was supposed to be the premier game of the season and it had proven a shabby affair.

Having had their photographs taken, pictures that would appear in every part of the globe over the next few days, the Wolves players showed the cup to the crowd before making their way back to the dressing room. But as they did so they were pelted with orange peel, apple cores and rubbish by the Rovers fans. It was a sad end to a difficult day for many of those involved.

Afterwards the match was roundly condemned in the national media. The long-departed *Sunday Pictorial* carried the headline "the dustbin final" and their reporter Laurie Pignon wrote: "There has never been a final like this one. I hope there is never one like it again. To me Wembley is more than a match between the season's giants. It's the Ascot of football, the glittering finale of the season. But this was just another shoddy match that could have been played at any time.

"The referee had annoyed everybody... Blackburn fans for allowing a Wolves goal, Wolves supporters for disallowing two. ...Wolves annoyed the crowd with their hard and sometimes foul tackling, a fault which Blackburn shared.

"But most of all I'm sure the fans were annoyed at having yet another Cup final ruined when Dave Whelan broke a leg. This morbid slow march with the stretcher is almost a permanent fixture on the Cup Final programme... the match was now a formality... in fairness to the teams and to the crowds there must be substitutes."

The loss of Whelan changed Bill Slater's mind about substitutes. "His injury convinced me of the need for them. Up until then I just thought players getting injured was simply part of the game, one you had to deal with and just roll your sleeves up and fight a little harder. After that I was in favour of substitutes and as I couldn't see it being restricted just for players being injured I thought the system allowing a substitute was the right one."

Substitutes were first allowed in the 1967 final between Spurs and Chelsea, but with neither Cliff Jones nor Joe Kirkup getting on, it wasn't until the following year when West Bromwich Albion's Dennis Clarke became the first ever Cup final sub, replacing John Kaye at the start of extra time.

Bill Slater says: "There was no way back for Blackburn after they were reduced to ten men.

The Final

The game died and we just used our extra man to tire them out. I went into the Rovers dressing room afterwards. I knew Ronnie Clayton very well from playing together with England. He was very down. I tried to cheer him up but never really succeeded."

Quite naturally the mood in the victorious dressing room was entirely different as players sipped champagne from the FA Cup. But if anyone thought Cullis would for once drop his guard and take part in the celebrations they should have known better.

Asked by photographers to be photographed drinking champagne from the cup he refused as he didn't drink it, and his offer to drink tea instead wasn't really what the cameramen were hoping for. Later, at the traditional post-match banquet, the manager, after saying as expected how it was a great honour to win the FA Cup, was already looking ahead to next season and reminded the players when pre-season training would get under way.

None of this came as a great surprise to George Showell. "I can't say I ever got to know Stan Cullis as he certainly never joined in with the lads and our activities – even on tour – and to be honest we wouldn't have wanted him to. He was still an excellent manager, though, and what upsets me is that today managers get knighthoods and OBEs a lot more easily than back then. Cullis was a truly great manager and yet he never even got an OBE."

It's a view Eddie Stuart supports: "He brought me over from South Africa and I remain ever so grateful as he gave me my big chance. He must have been the strictest manager of all time and I can recall one time when I was captain he gave me a right rollicking and I said to him that he didn't know what he was talking about.

"After the game he said I was to see him in his office on the Monday and it was the worst and longest weekend of my footballing career. When I got outside his office I was terrified about knocking on the door and going in – I got told off even after I said I'd made a mistake. He let you know he was the manager, but his success record was phenomenal so he certainly earned the right to feel that way.

"He made Wolves a hard outfit, but we were never dirty. Cullis loved to see a player making a good strong tackle but he would get angry – and he would let you know he was annoyed later – if any Wolves player took the player down from behind.

"Cullis's teams were always in the top three and I feel that his record has been overlooked when you hear commentators talk about great managers because, without taking anything away from the likes of Shankly, Busby, Clough and Ferguson I feel they all come second to Stan Cullis – and that's despite the fact that he never played me at Wembley!"

Bryan Douglas still cannot watch the FA Cup being presented at the end of each year's final. "The FA Cup final was my biggest disappointment in

The Final

football. Even to this day, after I have watched the final on television I have to switch it off at the end as I can't watch. The Cup final was the biggest sporting event in Britain every year, bigger even when the World Cup was on."

Faye MacLeod remembers: "The Cup Final, of course, was a big disappointment. Ally was voted man of the match but would have swapped that for a winner's medal. They never had a chance when Dave Whelan was taken off."

After the match it was a disappointed Rovers side that assembled for the official banquet. They were minus the injured Dave Whelan, who said from his hospital bed: "I feel as though I let the lads down. I went cleanly into the tackle but Deeley put out his foot late and I went over it."

Not surprisingly, Derek Dougan and his fiancée Valerie Martin left the banquet early. It seemed certain that he had played his last game for the club.

As a consequence he missed the after-dinner speeches in which the Blackburn chairman Norman Forbes made only a passing reference to the work of the manager Dally Duncan in getting the side to Wembley, preferring instead to pay a long tribute to the previous incumbent, Johnny Carey. In addition, Forbes also warned the players that they were expected to "pull their weight next season".

Three weeks later Duncan was dismissed.

Douglas was not surprised Duncan was sacked. "Carey was a better manager than Dally Duncan, who kept going on about what he'd done at Luton.

The players used to ask ourselves whether we were Luton or Blackburn! Duncan was a square peg in a round hole. Carey had moulded the team together, but when Duncan came along he didn't have the respect of the players; some of his team talks were comical."

Wolves, meanwhile, returned to a heroes' welcome before an 80,000 crowd that packed Wolverhampton the next day. Arriving by train, they were transported to the Town Hall to be met by the Mayor and Mayoress, Alderman Norman Bagley and Mrs Joan Bridgewater, before they emerged on the balcony to the cheers of the crowd.

Bill Slater then showed the FA Cup and said: "Sometimes there are some people who do not think we are the best team in the country, but we think we have the best supporters."

Wolves had won the FA Cup for the fourth time.

Appendix One

Through the rounds

Preliminary Round Results – September 5th 1959

Horsham 1-3 Hastings United; Nelson 0-0 Ashton United; R Ashton United 1-2 Nelson; Worthing 3-1 Eastbourne United; Woking 3-0 Epsom; Windsor & Eton 2-3 Aylesbury United; Rossendale United 4-4 Lytham; R Lytham 2-1 Rossendale United; Bromley 5-0 Redhill; South Liverpool 3-4 Pwllheli & District; Winsford United 0-3 Northwich Victoria; St Helens Town 0-2 Earlestown; Skelmersdale United 0-0 Mossley; R Mossley 3-0 Skelmersdale United; Wimbledon 6-0 Dorking; Witton Albion 3-3 Stalybridge Celtic; R Stalybridge Celtic 1-2 Witton Albion; Bognor Regis Town 1-2 Eastbourne; Lostock Gralam 0-1 Linotype & Machinery; Bromsgrove Rovers 2-1 Stafford Rangers; Cheltenham Town 1-0 Lovells Athletic; Maidenhead United 4-1 Huntley & Palmers; New Brighton 1-0 Marine; Erith & Belvedere 0-2 Tonbridge; Witney Town 0-1 Oxford City; Metropolitan Police 1-3 Carshalton Athletic; Bideford 4-3 Tavistock; Brentwood & Warley 1-2 Tilbury

Hayes 2-1 Wealdstone; Droylsden 2-1 Darwen; Betteshanger CW 2-2 Ramsgate Athletic; R Ramsgate Athletic 0-1 Betteshanger CW; Walton & Hersham 0-2 Kingstonian; Brush Sports 2-1 Long Eaton United; Chatham Town 0-3 Sheppey United; Littlehampton Town 1-2 Arundel; Lancing Athletic 2-1 Newhaven; Bilston 3-2 Lockheed Leamington; Stork 1-2 Runcorn; Aveley 1-2 Leytonstone; Stockton Heath 0-3 Congleton Town; Wokingham Town 5-2 Slough Town; Crawley Town 6-1 Southwick; Ford United 1-2 Hendon;
First Qualifying Round Results, September 19th 1959

Fifty Years On

Ely City 0-3 Cambridge United; Andover 0-0 Gosport Borough Ath; R Gosport Borough Ath 0-1 Andover; Clapton 2-4 Hornchurch & Upminster; Dartford 4-1 Sheppey United; Hastings United 4-1 Bexhill Town; Barking 0-1 Leytonstone; Farsley Celtic 5-2 Upton Colliery; Histon 1-4 Cambridge City; Nelson 2-2 Lytham; R Lytham 2-0 Nelson; Southall 1-0 Harrow Town; Sutton United 6-0 Leatherhead; Worthing 1-6 Crawley Town; Sheffield 2-3 Worksop Town; Ware 1-7 Enfield; Winchester City 1-4 Fareham Town; Woking 3-0 Dulwich Hamlet; Fleetwood 2-2 Clitheroe; R Clitheroe 1-0 Fleetwood; Taunton 7-0 Weston-Super-Mare; Marlow 0-3 Banbury Spencer; Macclesfield Town 2-3 Ellesmere Port Town; Hoddesdon Town 2-0 St Albans City; Gainsborough Trinity 4-1 Alford United; Scarborough 2-2 Ashington; R Ashington 0-0 Scarborough; R Scarborough 1-0 Ashington; Ilford 4-1 Rainham Town; Brierley Hill Alliance 2-2 Rugby Town; R Rugby Town 1-0 Brierley Hill Alliance; Buxton 4-1 Linotype & Machinery; Wellingborough Town 3-2 Rothwell Town; Dover 0-0 Betteshanger CW; R Betteshanger CW 3-1 Dover; Wellington Town 1-1 Oswestry Town;

R Oswestry Town 3-1 Wellington Town; Gresley Rovers 2-2 Atherstone Town; R Atherstone Town 2-0 Gresley Rovers; Kidderminster Harriers 7-1 Bournville Athletic; Bangor City 3-2 New Brighton; Aylesbury United 1-4 Oxford City; Lowestoft Town 6-2 Sheringham; Earlestown 5-2 Pwllheli & District; Glastonbury 2-1 Street; Staines Town 1-2 Hayes; Wimbledon 3-0 Bromley; Penrith 1-0 Morecambe; Altrincham 7-1 Droylsden; Witton Albion 2-1 Hyde United; Yiewsley 2-1 Uxbridge; Melksham Town 2-4 Trowbridge Town; Tow Law Town 2-1 Whitby Town; Gorleston 2-2 Diss Town; R Diss Town 1-2 Gorleston; Whitstable 1-6 Folkestone; Frickley Colliery 1-0 East End Park WMC; Grays Athletic 2-1 Tilbury; Devizes Town 3-2 Chippenham United; Horwich RMI 1-2 Bacup Borough; Brigg Town 1-1 Ashby Institute; R Ashby Institute 1-5 Brigg Town; Halesowen Town 2-4 Bilston; Ebbw Vale 2-2 Barry Town; R Barry Town 6-1 Ebbw Vale; Congleton Town 0-3 Northwich Victoria; Cradley Heath 0-5 Stourbridge; Bourne Town 4-1 Louth United; Runcorn 3-2 Llandudno; Rushden Town 3-2 Stamford; Warminster Town 1-1 Frome Town; R

Appendix One

Frome Town 1-2 Warminster Town; Selby Town 1-3 Denaby United; Hertford Town 7-0 Cheshunt; Letchworth Town 5-0 Dunstable Town; Westbury United 3-1 Chippenham Town; Retford Town 2-2 Heanor Town; R Heanor Town 4-0 Retford Town; Portland United 2-3 Salisbury; Newmarket Town 1-4 Clacton Town; Carshalton Athletic 2-4 Kingstonian; Ferryhill Athletic 0-0 Bridlington Town; R Bridlington Town 1-2 Ferryhill Athletic; Cowes 2-0 Newport (IOW); Yorkshire Amateur 1-3 Goole Town; Norton Woodseats 2-1 Boots Athletic; Consett 2-1 Evenwood Town; Abingdon Town 1-1 Maidenhead United; R Maidenhead United 3-1 Abingdon Town; Stevenage Town 0-1 Vauxhall Motors (Luton); Gloucester City 1-3 Cheltenham Town; Prescot Cables 4-0 Flint Town United; Thetford Town 2-4 Great Yarmouth Town; Romford (2) 1-3 Finchley; Horden CW 2-2 North Shields; R North Shields 3-1 Horden CW; Chatteris Town 1-2 March Town United; Bexleyheath & Welling 5-1 Sittingbourne; Stowmarket 0-3 Sudbury Town; Hounslow Town 6-0 Wembley; Shotton CW 0-2 Spennymoor United

Deal Town 0-1 Ashford Town; Haywards Heath 3-3 Eastbourne; R Eastbourne 4-2 Haywards Heath; Tamworth 2-2 Ilkeston Town; R Ilkeston Town 2-1 Tamworth; Moor Green 2-4 Bromsgrove Rovers; Billingham Synthonia 3-5 Murton CW; South Normanton MW 3-0 Ransome & Marles; Milnthorpe Corinthians 0-3 Netherfield (Kendal); Lancaster City 2-4 Burscough; Edgware Town 0-1 Hendon; Woodford Town 1-1 Leyton; R Leyton 1-0 Woodford Town; Gravesend & Northfleet 2-0 Tonbridge; Basingstoke Town 5-2 Alton Town; Whitton United 1-2 Harwich & Parkeston; Stonehouse 0-5 Llanelli; Hinckley Athletic 0-1 Brush Sports; Lancing Athletic 2-3 Arundel; Mossley 2-1 Chorley; Canterbury City 1-0 Snowdown CW; Cinderford Town 1-1 Merthyr Tydfil; R Merthyr Tydfil 2-0 Cinderford Town; Stocksbridge Works 1-3 Matlock Town; Wolverton Town & BR 2-1 Hitchin Town; Bridgwater Town (1) 2-1 Minehead; Wadebridge Town 3-2 St Blazey; Burton Albion 1-4 Nuneaton Borough; Dagenham 1-1 Walthamstow Avenue; R Walthamstow Avenue 4-0 Dagenham; Tunbridge Wells United 1-1 Maidstone United (1); R Maidstone United (1) 2-3 Tunbridge Wells United; Penzance 3-5 Bideford;

Fifty Years On

Shirebrook MW 1-1 Sutton Town; R Sutton Town 3-4 Shirebrook MW; Sutton Coldfield Town 2-3 Hednesford Town; St Neots Town 1-1 Holbeach United; R Holbeach United 3-2 St Neots Town; Wokingham Town 4-1 Chesham United; Evesham United 2-0 Bedworth Town; Skegness Town 5-0 Grantham

Second Qualifying Round – October 3rd 1959

The second qualifying round saw Hoddesdon Town thrashed 15-0 by Enfield whilst in a thrilling game Bury Town only just overcame Clacton Town 6-5. Wimbledon's hopes were dashed when Sutton United beat them 1-0.

Enfield 15-0 Hoddesdon Town; Ashford Town 1-0 Folkestone; Dartford 0-2 Tunbridge Wells United; Poole Town 4-0 Bridport; Southall 1-1 Yiewsley; R Yiewsley 1-2 Southall; Taunton 0-0 Glastonbury; R Glastonbury 2-1 Taunton; Northwich Victoria 0-3 Ellesmere Port Town; Clitheroe 6-3 Penrith; Gainsborough Trinity 4-1 Bourne Town; Stockton 4-2 Stanley United; Buxton 1-2 Witton Albion; Wellingborough Town 0-2 Rushden Town; Kidderminster Harriers 0-2 Oswestry Town; Oxford City 5-1 Banbury Spencer; Leytonstone 1-3 Leyton; Bangor City 4-1 Runcorn; Harwich & Parkeston 4-2 Sudbury Town; Denaby United 2-0 Farsley Celtic; Great Yarmouth Town 6-2 Lowestoft Town; Earlestown 0-1 Prescot Cables; Shildon 4-0 Redcar Albion; Spennymoor United 3-1 South Bank; Wimbledon 0-1 Sutton United; Annfield Plain 4-1 Bedlington Mechanics; Altrincham 3-2 Mossley; Atherstone Town 0-2 Ilkeston Town

    Tow Law Town 4-4 West Auckland Town; R West Auckland Town 5-2 Tow Law Town; Bromsgrove Rovers 4-0 Stourbridge; Frickley Colliery 1-3 Goole Town; Grays Athletic 2-2 Ilford; R Ilford 2-4 Grays Athletic; Willington 4-1 Whitley Bay; Cheltenham Town 2-2 Merthyr Tydfil; R Merthyr Tydfil 0-1 Cheltenham Town; Brigg Town 0-3 Skegness Town; Maidenhead United 5-0 Wokingham

Appendix One

Town; Kingstonian 0-3 Woking; Matlock Town 3-1 Worksop Town; Warminster Town 0-5 Salisbury; Spalding United 1-2 Corby Town; Westbury United 1-3 Trowbridge Town; Creswell Colliery 2-5 Heanor Town; Calne & Harris Utd. 7-2 Devizes Town; Walthamstow Avenue 4-0 Finchley; Lytham 2-1 Bacup Borough; Ferryhill Athletic 2-4 Consett; Cowes 3-0 Andover; Bishop's Stortford 0-1 Hertford Town; Bideford 6-2 Truro City; Murton CW 2-5 Scarborough; Hayes 1-0 Hounslow Town; North Shields 5-0 Newburn; Easington CW 0-2 Boldon CW; Bury Town 6-5 Clacton Town; Betteshanger CW 6-0 Canterbury City; South Normanton MW 6-1 Shirebrook MW; Bungay Town 1-0 Gorleston; Barry Town 2-0 Llanelli; Hendon 0-2 Hornchurch & Upminster; Gravesend & Northfleet 4-3 Bexleyheath & Welling; Basingstoke Town 4-1 Fareham Town; Brush Sports 4-3 Nuneaton Borough; Biggleswade Town 1-2 Letchworth Town; Burscough 4-1 Netherfield (Kendal); Ilminster Town 1-3 Bridgwater Town (1); Barnstaple Town 9-1 Wadebridge Town; Bilston 5-1 Rugby Town; Wolverton Town & BR 5-1 Vauxhall Motors (Luton); Arundel 2-5 Hastings United; Cambridge City 5-1 March Town United; Cambridge United 3-0 Holbeach United; Belper Town 3-2 Norton Woodseats; Crawley Town 2-2 Eastbourne; R Eastbourne 1-2 Crawley Town; Evesham United 3-1 Hednesford Town

Third Qualifying Round – October 17th 1959

With teams now within touching distance of giant-killing opportunities there were some keen matches, with Rushden Town, Hayes and Sutton United beating near neighbours Corby Town, Southall and Woking respectively after replays. Cambridge City also won a tight derby match 1-0 at local rivals United. Still, at least this defeat for the United fans was better than in 1946 when United had eight goals without reply put into their net by City, which remains their record cup defeat.

Ashford Town 3-0 Betteshanger CW; Poole Town 0-1 Salisbury; Southall 1-1 Hayes; R Hayes 4-1 Southall; Sutton United 3-3 Woking; R Woking 1-3 Sutton ; Leyton 1-1 Grays Athletic; R Grays Athletic 6-2 Leyton; Clitheroe 1-2 Burscough; Stockton 1-1 Spennymoor United; R Spennymoor United 1-0 Stockton; Heanor Town 2-1 South Normanton MW; Oxford City 3-0 Maidenhead United; Shildon 2-0 North Shields; Goole Town 0-1 Denaby United; Annfield Plain 2-3 Scarborough; Willington 0-2 West Auckland Town; Oswestry Town 3-1 Bromsgrove Rovers; Hertford Town 2-3 Enfield; Letchworth Town 3-2 Wolverton Town & BR; Ellesmere Port Town 4-1 Witton Albion; Calne & Harris Utd. 1-6 Trowbridge Town; Walthamstow Avenue 7-1 Hornchurch & Upminster; Lytham 1-1 Altrincham; R Altrincham 3-0 Lytham; Prescot Cables 4-1 Bangor City; Bury Town 2-0 Harwich & Parkeston; Bungay Town 1-4 Great Yarmouth Town; Barry Town 1-4 Cheltenham Town; Basingstoke Town 2-1 Cowes; Ilkeston Town 1-1 Brush Sports; R Brush Sports 1-2 Ilkeston Town; Barnstaple Town 1-1 Bideford; R Bideford 1-5 Barnstaple Town; Skegness Town 0-0 Gainsborough Trinity; R Gainsborough Trinity 3-0 Skegness Town; Boldon CW 0-4 Consett; Bridgwater Town (1) 3-1 Glastonbury; Corby Town 2-2 Rushden Town; R Rushden Town 2-1 Corby Town; Tunbridge Wells United 0-3 Gravesend & Northfleet; Cambridge United 0-1 Cambridge City; Belper Town 2-3 Matlock Town; Crawley Town 2-2 Hastings United; R Hastings United 5-2 Crawley Town; Evesham United 2-1 Bilston

Fourth qualifying round – 31st October 1959

With 30 places up for grabs in the first round proper sixty teams took part in the fourth and final qualifying round on Halloween 1959.

There was disappointment for north-east non-league giants Bishop Auckland, beaten by Scarborough 2-1 at home, who were bidding to qualify for the first round for the sixth consecutive season. The

Appendix One

Bishops had beaten Second Division side Ipswich Town in the 1954–55 third round before falling to York City from Division 3 North in the fourth. Bishop had first entered the FA Cup in 1889–90, but are better known for their FA Amateur Cup successes, winning the competition ten times, including a hat-trick of successes between 1955 and 1957.

There was, however, success for Bishops' local rivals West Auckland Town, who finally made it though to the first round proper for the first time ever by overcoming Durham City 4-1 in a replay. West had first taken part in the FA Cup in 1905–06. Although they never won the FA Amateur Cup, their best effort being in 1960–61 when they lost in the final at Wembley to Walthamstow Avenue 2-1, West did win the Sir Thomas Lipton Trophy in 1909 and 1911. This was one of the first international football competitions and earned West the title of 'World Champions', as featured in a 1981 Television Movie starring Dennis Waterman and entitled *A Captain's Tale*.

Also in the north-east, local rivals Consett and ex-league club South Shields took four games to sort out who would play Chesterfield in the first round proper, with the second replay ending 5-5 after extra-time. Eventually, 'the Mariners', as Shields are known, won through by a single Don Robson goal in the fourth game that was played at Appleby Park, home of North Shields.

Wigan Athletic crashed out of the competition, losing 3-1 after a replay at Rhyl. Formed in 1932,

Fifty Years On

Wigan first entered the FA Cup at the start of the 1933–34 season and the following season made it through to the FA Cup proper for the first time, going out 4-1 to Millwall at home in the third round but not before hammering Carlisle United from Division 3 North 6-1 away.

In the 1953–54 FA Cup Wigan beat Southern League side Hereford United 4-1 at home on December 12th 1953, a match watched at Springfield Park by Wigan's record crowd of 27,256 and a figure that remains the record FA Cup attendance for a match between two non-League teams at a non-league ground.

Further south, Yeovil were given no opportunity to add to their collection of League 'scalps' when Bath City won 2-0 at Huish Park. Bury Town's bid for glory also ended when Peterborough beat them 7-1 at London Road. There were 9,922 in attendance, demonstrating the pull that the FA Cup had for the public in 1959.

Enfield 3-0 Rushden Town; Sutton United 2-3 Hastings United; Weymouth 0-1 Dorchester Town; Yeovil Town 0-2 Bath City; Gainsborough Trinity 4-2 Heanor Town; Bishop Auckland 1-2 Scarborough; Wycombe Wanderers 1-0 Oxford City; Shildon 6-1 Denaby United; West Auckland Town 2-2 Durham City; R Durham City 0-0 West Auckland Town; R West Auckland Town 4-1 Durham City; Worcester City 0-3 Hereford United; Blyth Spartans 4-0 Spennymoor United; Bedford Town (1) 5-3 Hayes; Grays Athletic 1-3 Chelmsford City; Margate 1-0 Guildford City; Cheltenham Town 0-0 Bridgwater Town (1); R Bridgwater Town (1) 0-1 Cheltenham Town; Oswestry Town 4-1 Evesham United; Letchworth Town 3-4 King's Lynn; Ellesmere Port Town 1-2 Burscough; Walthamstow Avenue 2-1 Great Yarmouth

Appendix One

Town; Kettering Town 1-0 Boston United; Consett 0-0
South Shields (2); R South Shields (2) 2-2 Consett; R
Consett 5-5 South Shields (2); R South Shields (2) 1-0
Consett; Prescot Cables 1-0 Altrincham; Tooting & Mitcham
United 1-2 Wisbech Town; Wigan Athletic 1-1 Rhyl; R Rhyl
3-1 Wigan Athletic; Peterborough United 7-1 Bury Town;
Gravesend & Northfleet 1-2 Ashford Town; Salisbury 2-2
Basingstoke Town; R Basingstoke Town 1-2 Salisbury;
Ilkeston Town 2-6 Matlock Town; Barnstaple Town 1-0
Trowbridge Town; Cambridge City 2-3 Headington United

First Round – November 14th 1959

Enfield 4-3 Headington United; Darlington 4-0 Prescot
Cables; Hastings United 1-2 Notts County; Bath City 3-1
Millwall; Bury 5-0 Hartlepools United; Dorchester Town 1-2
Port Vale; Rochdale 2-2 Carlisle United; R Carlisle United
1-3 Rochdale; Swindon Town 2-3 Walsall; Doncaster
Rovers 3-3 Gainsborough Trinity; R Gainsborough Trinity
0-1 Doncaster Rovers; Wrexham 2-1 Blyth Spartans;
Tranmere Rovers 0-1 Chester; Wycombe Wanderers 4-2
Wisbech Town; Accrington Stanley 1-2 Mansfield Town;
Barnsley 3-3 Bradford City; R Bradford City 2-1 Barnsley;
Brentford 5-0 Ashford Town; Crook Town 2-2 Matlock
Town; R Matlock Town 0-1 Crook Town ; Coventry City 1-1
Southampton; R Southampton 5-1 Coventry City; King's
Lynn 3-1 Aldershot; Rhyl 1-2 Grimsby Town; Norwich
City   1-1 Reading; R Reading 2-1 Norwich City; Shildon
1-1 Oldham Athletic; R Oldham Athletic 3-0 Shildon; West
Auckland Town 2-6 Stockport County; Crystal Palace 5-1
Chelmsford City; Southend United 6-0 Oswestry Town;
Bradford Park Avenue 6-1 Scarborough; Exeter City
4-0 Barnstaple Town; Bedford Town (1) 0-4 Gillingham;
Newport County 4-2 Hereford United; Cheltenham Town
0-0 Watford; R Watford 3-0 Cheltenham Town; Southport
2-2 Workington; R Workington 3-0 Southport; Torquay
United 7-1 Northampton Town; Walthamstow Avenue 2-3
Bournemouth; York City 3-1 Barrow; Kettering Town 1-1
Margate; R Margate 3-2 Kettering Town; Gateshead 3-4
Halifax Town; Peterborough United 4-3 Shrewsbury Town;
South Shields (2) 2-1 Chesterfield; Colchester United 2-3

Fifty Years On

Queen's Park Rangers; Salisbury 1-0 Barnet; Burscough 1-3 Crewe Alexandra;

Second Round – December 5th 1959
The second round of the FA Cup is one of the biggest matches of the season. Clubs know that if they can get through they will be in the pot with top-flight sides such as Manchester United and Spurs.

Enfield 1-5 Bournemouth; Bury 2-1 Oldham Athletic; Rochdale 1-1 Bradford City; R Bradford City 2-1 Rochdale; Southampton 3-0 Southend United; Watford 5-1 Wycombe Wanderers; Reading 4-2 King's Lynn; Walsall 2-3 Peterborough United; Gillingham 2-2 Torquay United; R Torquay United 1-2 Gillingham; Notts County 0-1 Bath City; Grimsby Town 2-3 Wrexham; Doncaster Rovers 3-2 Darlington; Stockport County 0-0 Crewe Alexandra; R Crewe Alexandra 2-0 Stockport County; Queen's Park Rangers 3-3 Port Vale; R Port Vale 2-1 Queen's Park Rangers; Crook Town 0-1 York City; Exeter City 3-1 Brentford; Mansfield Town 2-0 Chester; Margate 0-0 Crystal Palace; R Crystal Palace 3-0 Margate; Workington 1-0 Halifax Town; South Shields (2) 1-5 Bradford Park Avenue; Salisbury 0-1 Newport County

Third round – January 9th 1960
Blackpool 3-0 Mansfield Town; Bournemouth 1-0 York City; Bath City 0-1 Brighton & Hove Albion; Bristol City 2-3 Charlton Athletic; Bury 1-1 Bolton Wanderers; R Bolton Wanderers 4-2 Bury; Liverpool 2-1 Leyton Orient; Watford 2-1 Birmingham City; Gillingham 1-4 Swansea Town; Nottingham Forest 1-0 Reading; Aston Villa 2-1 Leeds United; Sheffield Wednesday 2-1 Middlesbrough; Crewe Alexandra 2-0 Workington; West Bromwich Albion 3-2 Plymouth Argyle; Sunderland 1-1 Blackburn Rovers; R Blackburn Rovers 4-1 Sunderland; Derby County 2-4 Manchester United; Lincoln City 1-1 Burnley; R Burnley 2-0 Lincoln City; Wrexham 1-2 Leicester City; Sheffield

Appendix One

United 3-0 Portsmouth; Ipswich Town 2-3 Peterborough United; Newcastle United 2-2 Wolverhampton Wanderers; R Wolverhampton Wanderers 4-2 Newcastle United; Manchester City 1-5 Southampton; Fulham 5-0 Hull City; Bristol Rovers 0-0 Doncaster Rovers; R Doncaster Rovers 1-2 Bristol Rovers; Bradford City 3-0 Everton; Chelsea 5-1 Bradford Park Avenue; Exeter City 1-2 Luton Town; Scunthorpe United 1-0 Crystal Palace; Huddersfield Town 1-1 West Ham United; R West Ham United 1-5 Huddersfield Town; Cardiff City 0-2 Port Vale; Newport County 0-4 Tottenham Hotspur; Stoke City 1-1 Preston North End; R Preston North End 3-1 Stoke City; Rotherham United 2-2 Arsenal; R Arsenal 1-1 Rotherham United; R Rotherham United 2-0 Arsenal

Fourth Round – January 30th 1960
Liverpool 1-3 Manchester United; Southampton 2-2 Watford; R Watford 1-0 Southampton; Leicester City 2-1 Fulham; Blackburn Rovers 1-1 Blackpool; R Blackpool 0-3 Blackburn Rovers; Sheffield Wednesday 2-0 Peterborough United; Wolverhampton Wanderers 2-1 Charlton Athletic; Crewe Alexandra 2-2 Tottenham Hotspur; R Tottenham Hotspur 13-2 Crewe Alexandra; West Bromwich Albion 2-0 Bolton Wanderers; Sheffield United 3-0 Nottingham Forest; Bristol Rovers 3-3 Preston North End; R Preston North End 5-1 Bristol Rovers; Bradford City 3-1 Bournemouth; Chelsea 1-2 Aston Villa; Scunthorpe United 0-1 Port Vale; Huddersfield Town 0-1 Luton Town; Swansea Town 0-0 Burnley; R Burnley 2-1 Swansea Town; Rotherham United 1-1 Brighton & Hove Albion; R Brighton & Hove Albion 1-1 Rotherham United; R Rotherham United 0-6 Brighton & Hove Albion

Fifth Round – February 20th 1960
Preston North End 2-1 Brighton & Hove Albion; Leicester City 2-1 West Bromwich Albion; Luton Town 1-4 Wolverhampton Wanderers; Sheffield United 3-2 Watford; Tottenham Hotspur 1-3 Blackburn Rovers; Manchester United 0-1 Sheffield Wednesday; Bradford City 2-2 Burnley;

Fifty Years On

R Burnley 5-0 Bradford City; Port Vale 1-2 Aston Villa

Quarter-finals – March 12th 1960
Leicester 1-2 Wolves; Burnley 3-3 Blackburn; R Blackburn 2-0 Burnley; Sheffield United 0-2 Sheffield Wednesday; Aston Villa 2-0 Preston North End

Appendix Two

Blackburn and Wolves team line-ups, FA Cup 1959–60

Blackburn Rovers

At Roker Park v Sunderland: Leyland, Bray, Whelan, Clayton, Woods, McGrath, Douglas, Dobing, Dougan, Vernon, MacLeod.

Replay: Leyland, Bray, Whelan, Clayton, Woods, McGrath, Bimpson, Douglas, Dougan, Vernon, MacLeod.

At Ewood Park v Blackpool: Leyland, Bray, Whelan, Clayton, Woods, McGrath, Douglas, Dobing, Dougan, Vernon, Macleod

Replay: Leyland, Bray, Whelan, Clayton, Woods, McGrath, Bimpson, Dobing, Dougan, Douglas, Macleod

At White Hart Lane v Tottenham Hotspur: Leyland, Bray, Whelan, Clayton, Woods, McGrath, Bimpson, Dobing, Dougan, Douglas, Macleod

Fifty Years On

At Turf Moor v Burnley: Leyland, Bray, Whelan, Clayton, Woods, McGrath, Bimpson, Dobing, Dougan, Douglas, Macleod

Replay: Leyland, Bray, Whelan, Clayton, Woods, McGrath, Bimpson, Dobing, Dougan, Douglas, Macleod

Semi-final v Sheffield Wednesday at Maine Road: Leyland, Bray, Whelan, Clayton, Woods, McGrath, Bimpson, Dobing, Dougan, Douglas, Macleod

Final: Leyland, Bray, Whelan, Clayton, Woods, McGrath, Bimpson, Dobing, Dougan, Douglas, Macleod

Appearances
9 – Leyland, Bray, Whelan, Clayton, Woods, McGrath, Douglas, Dougan, MacLeod; 8 – Dobing; 7 – Bimpson; 3 – Vernon

Scorers
Dobing 5, Bimpson 3, Dougan 3, McGrath 2, Vernon 2, Macleod 2, Douglas 1, Woods 1

Wolverhampton Wanderers

At St James' Park v Newcastle United: Finlayson, Stuart, Harris, Clamp, Slater, Flowers, Deeley, Mason, Murray, Broadbent, Horne

Appendix Two

Replay: Finlayson, Stuart, Harris, Clamp, Slater, Flowers, Deeley, Mason, Murray, Broadbent, Horne

At Molineux v Charlton Athletic: Finlayson, Stuart, Harris, Clamp, Slater, Flowers, Deeley, Mason, Murray, Broadbent, Horne

At Kenilworth Road v Luton Town: Sidebottom, Stuart, Harris, Clamp, Slater, Flowers, Deeley, Mason, Murray, Broadbent, Horne

At Filbert Street v Leicester City: Sidebottom, Showell, Harris, Clamp, Slater, Flowers, Deeley, Mason, Stobart, Broadbent, Horne

Semi final v Aston Villa at The Hawthorns: Finlayson, Showell, Harris, Clamp, Slater, Flowers, Mannion, Mason, Murray, Broadbent, Deeley

Final: Finlayson, Stuart, Harris, Clamp, Slater, Flowers, Deeley, Stobart, Murray, Broadbent, Horne

Appearances
7 – Harris, Clamp, Slater, Flowers, Deeley, Broadbent; 6 – Murray, Mason, Horne; 5 – Finlayson; 4 – Stuart; 3 – Showell; 2 – Sidebottom, Stobart; 1 – Mannion

Scorers
Deeley 4, Clamp 2, Flowers 2, Mason 2, Murray 2, Broadbent 2, Horne 2, own goals 2

Appendix Three

Previous appearances of Wolves and Blackburn in the FA Cup final

Blackburn Rovers
1881–82 – Lost
Round 1
Blackburn Park Road H 9-1
Brown 2, J Douglas, Wilson og, Avery, J Hargreaves, Strachan 2, AN Other (og)
Round 2
Bolton Wanderers H 6-2
Avery, McIntyre 2, Brown 2, Sharples
Round 3
Bye
Round 4
Darwen H 5-1 J Hargreaves 2, Brown, J Duckworth 2
Quarter-final
Wednesbury Old Athletic H 3-1 Lofthouse, Avery, Strachan
Semi-final
The Wednesday 0-0
Played at St John's Rugby Club, Huddersfield, March 6th 1882
Semi-final replay
The Wednesday 5-1

175

J Hargreaves, Avery, J Douglas, Suter, own goal
Played at Whalley Range, Manchester March 15th 1882
Final
Old Etonians 0-1
Macauley 8 mins
Played at Kennington Oval, March 25th 1882
Blackburn: Roger Howarth, Hugh McIntyre, Fergus Suter, capt – Freddie Hargreaves, Harold Sharples, Jack Hargreaves, Geoffrey Avery, James Brown, Thomas Strachan, Jimmy Douglas, John Duckworth
Old Etonians: John Frederick Peel Rawlinson, Thomas French, Percy de Paravicini, capt – Hon Arthur Kinnaird, Charles Foley, Philip Novelli, Arthur Tempest Blakiston Dunn, Reginald Heber Macauley, Harry Chester Goodhart, John Chevallier, William Anderson

Rovers travelled south after a wonderful season in which in all matches they had won 31 and drawn five. One of these was the semi-final match with The Wednesday, played at St John's Rugby Club, Huddersfield, with the aim of popularising football in a rugby stronghold. In the replay Rovers came from a goal down to win 5-1 and although they were up against the celebrated Old Etonians, led by Lord Kinnaird, they were regarded as slight favourites.

There were an estimated 1,000 of their followers in a crowd of 6,000.

The following edited highlights are taken mainly from the *Preston Herald* report.

Appendix Three

Rovers' Strachan kicked off the match at precisely 3.00pm. However, it was Old Etonians who were quickest into their stride and the Lancastrian side were grateful to some brilliant defending by Suter to prevent Dunn and Macauley from opening the scoring. The Blackburn back then earned the plaudits of the onlookers by magnificently tackling Novelli, who was racing towards the goal at train speed. However, the southern side were not to be denied and opened the scoring on eight minutes. It followed fine approach play by Brown and Anderson that was taken on by Dunn who looked to be offside. When the left winger found Macauley he beat Howarth with a long shot.

Rovers might have equalised but Strachan was just unable to keep his header down. Yet this was a rare attack by Blackburn during the first period and they would no doubt have been relieved to have gone in just a goal down at half-time, especially after French missed a clear opening to double the Old Etonians' advantage.

Disaster, however, was just around the corner when Avery was charged down and Rovers were reduced to ten fully fit men. The injury appears to have been one of many suffered by Blackburn's players during the match and there was criticism of the victors' approach afterwards by some reporters.

Despite such a disadvantage, Rovers emerged after the break clearly determined to get back into the match, and Rawlinson was forced to make a fine save from a Douglas shot. Numerous crosses from Douglas on the right and Hargreaves on the left were rained down on the Etonians defence in which Kinnaird and Foley at half-back were outstanding. Rovers, urged on by their supporters in the last half hour of the match, looked as if they would equalise when Duckworth was presented with a glorious opportunity. But with only the keeper to beat he hit a feeble shot that was easily saved. Despite the result, when Rovers players arrived back in the town on the following Tuesday evening thousands were out in force to applaud their efforts.

This represented the last hurrah of the amateur in the FA Cup. The game's man of the match, Scotsman Fergus Suter, was arguably the first professional footballer. A stonemason by trade, he had played for Partick Thistle and Rangers before moving to England in 1878 to play for Darwen only to discover, he claimed, that English stone was too difficult to work. In 1880 Blackburn Rovers secured his service, resulting in considerable tension between the two east Lancashire clubs. With no visible means of support, Suter was able to keep himself remarkably fit, fuelling criticism that he was being paid to play.

1883–84 – Won
Round 1
Southport H 7-0
J Douglas 2, Lofthouse, J Duckworth, Sowerbutts, Avery 2
Round 2
South Shore A 7-0
Avery 2, Suter, J Sowerbutts 2, J Douglas, McIntyre

Appendix Three

Round 3
Padiham H 3-0
Brown, Connell – og, Strachan
Round 4
Staveley H 5-1 Brown 4, Sowerbutts
Quarter-final
Upton Park A 3-0
Inglis, Lofthouse 2
Semi-final
Notts County 1-0
Lofthouse
Played at Aston Lower Grounds, Birmingham, March 1st 1884
Final
Queen's Park, Glasgow 2-1
Blackburn: Sowerbutts 30, Forrest 35
Queen's Park: Christie 41
Played at Kennington Oval, March 29th 1884
Blackburn: Herbie Arthur, Fergus Suter, Joseph Beverley, capt – Hugh McIntyre, James Forrest, Jack Hargreaves, James Brown, Jock Inglis, Joe Sowerbutts, Jimmy Douglas, Joseph Lofthouse
Queen's Park: George Gillespie, John MacDonald, Walter Arnott, John Gow, capt – Charles Campbell, David Allan, William Harrower, Dr John Smith, William Anderson, William Watt, Robert Christie

Glasgow's Queen's Park were the first club from Scotland to take part in the FA Cup, drawing with the Wanderers in the semi-finals of the inaugural competition in 1871–72. However, with the replay fixed to be played at Kennington Oval, Queen's Park were forced to withdraw as they didn't possess the funds to cover their travel and accommodation. In 1883–84 they had had a magnificent run to the final, in which they had scored 43 goals and conceded just three in six games, and during which they overcame the holders, Blackburn Olympic, 4-1 in the semi-final.

Unlike in 1882 Rovers were in their normal light blue and white strip while the Scots wore their black and white striped jerseys. Queen's Park were regarded by the bookmakers as favourites and they started by far the brighter, dazzling the Lancastrians with clever dribbling and quick passing. Yet Rovers refused to yield and few chances of any real quality were created. With the match becoming something of a stalemate it broke into life on the half-hour mark when Brown, receiving the ball from Forrest, took it round Arnott and MacDonald before beating Gillespie and pulling the ball back for Sowerbutts to push it into the empty goal (goal nets were still seven years away from being introduced).

Blackburn went two ahead when Forrest belted home a left-wing cross. Queen's Park got themselves back into the match on 41 minutes when Christie got possession and drilled a shot that Arthur was unable to stop. The Scottish side pushed forward in search of an equaliser as soon as the match got under way after half-time, but it was Blackburn who created the better chances and there was a dispute when Gillespie appeared to have dropped a shot from Brown over the line that would have made it 2-2. Brown then

Appendix Three

drove a shot under the bar but was clearly offside. Queen's Park might have equalised late on but when the referee, Major Marindin, blew the final whistle the only Scots taking a winner's medal home were the three in the Rovers line-up.

Source – *The Accrington Times* – Saturday April 5th 1884

1884–85 – Won
Round 1
Rossendale H 11-0
Fecitt 4, Barton 3, Sowerbutts 2, Brown, A Birtwistle
(Record FA Cup victory for Blackburn Rovers)
Round 2
Blackburn Olympic 3-2
Fecitt 2, Sowerbutts
Round 3
Witton H 5-1
Forrest, Brown, Sowerbutts, Lofthouse, Fecitt
Round 4
Romford (1876) H 8-0
Fecitt 2, Rostron, J Douglas, Sowerbutts 2, og 2
Round 5
Bye
Quarter-final
WBA A 2-0
Lofthouse, J Douglas
Semi-final
Old Carthusians 5-1
Brown 2, Sowerbutts 2, Lofthouse
Played at Trent Bridge, Nottingham, March 7th 1885

Final
Queen's Park, Glasgow 2-0
Forrest 14, Brown 58
Played at Kennington Oval, April 4th 1885
Blackburn: Herbie Arthur, Richard Turner, Fergus Suter, George Haworth, Hugh McIntyre, James Forrest, Joe Sowerbutts, Joseph Lofthouse, Jimmy Douglas, capt – James Brown, Howard Fecitt
Queen's Park: George Gillespie, Walter Arnott, William MacLeod, John MacDonald, capt – Charles Campbell, William Sellar, William Anderson, N McWhammel Alexander Hamilton, David Allan, Woodville Gray.

The final was a repeat of the previous season, only this time the Scots did not score. Queen's Park's clever passing that had confused Rovers in the first period of the 1884 final was not as conspicuous this time and the result was that the Lancastrians were comfortable winners.

The match was watched by what was believed to be the largest football crowd that had ever assembled in London – more than 12,000.

Brown, the Rovers captain, hit the bar on 14 minutes and as it rebounded Forrest was quickest to react and drove home the opening goal, thus scoring for a second consecutive year. Victory was ensured on 70 minutes when Fecitt and Forrest opened up the Scottish defence for Brown to drive home.

Appendix Three

1885–86 – Won
Round 1
Clitheroe A 2-0
J Douglas AN other
Round 2
Oswaldtwistle Rovers H 1-0
McIntyre
Round 3
Darwen Old Wanderers H 6-1
Sowerbutts 2, Brown 2, Fecitt, Lofthouse
Round 4
Staveley H 7-1
Lofthouse 2, Fecitt 2, Walton 2, Sowerbutts
Round 5
Bye
Quarter-final
Brentwood A 3-1
Fecitt, Walton 2
Semi-final
Swifts 2-1
Walton, Strachan
Played at Derby Cricket Ground, March 13th 1886
Final
Blackburn 0 WBA 0
Played at Kennington Oval, April 3rd 1886
Final Replay
Blackburn 2 WBA 0
Sowerbutts 5, Brown 73
Played at Derby Racecourse Ground, April 10th 1886

Two matches were needed, but by the end of the replay Blackburn Rovers had become the second side

Fifty Years On

to win the FA Cup in three consecutive seasons, the Wanderers having first achieved the feat between 1876 and 1878.

The first match was, like many finals that followed it, a poor affair, tension often winning out over skill. It was no great surprise that no goals were scored and when referee Major Marindin consulted both teams on their willingness to play an extra half-hour Blackburn declined, so poorly had they played. Better to take a chance in the second match, they reckoned, and so it proved when the teams met a week later at the Racecourse Ground in Derby before a 15,000 crowd in which the Rovers fans were heavily outnumbered by their West Brom counterparts.

Initially this seemed to inspire the side from the Black Country but after just five minutes Sowerbutts scored for the second time in an FA Cup final after he broke through the West Brom defence to fire home. The same player then looked to have doubled the lead, only to be ruled offside, but there was to be no stopping Brown in the second half when picking the ball up just inside the opposing half he showed electrifying pace and then, steadying himself just outside the area, flashed an unstoppable shot past Turner. By doing so Jimmy Brown became the first and only player to score in three consecutive FA Cup finals even if one of them was in a replay.

Having scored such a wonderful goal it was perhaps appropriate that it was Brown who was presented with the winning trophy, which was handed to him by Major Marindin. In recognition of that third victory Blackburn were presented with a beautiful silver shield after the Wanderers, at the time of their third consecutive success in 1878, had agreed to hand back the trophy on condition that it was to be a challenge trophy in perpetuity.

Blackburn: Herbie Arthur, Richard Turner, Fergus Suter, Joseph Heyes, Hugh McIntyre, James Forrest, Jimmy Douglas, Thomas Strachan, Joe Sowerbutts, Howard Fecitt, capt – James Brown
West Bromwich Albion: Bob Roberts, Harry Green, Harry Bell, Ezra Horton, Charlie Perry, George Timmins, George Woodhall, Tom Green, capt – Jimmy Bayliss, Arthur Loach, George Bell

Replay
Blackburn: Herbie Arthur, Richard Turner, Fergus Suter, Nat Walton, Jimmy Forrest, Hugh McIntyre, Jimmy Douglas, Thomas Strachan, Joe Sowerbutts, Howard Fecitt, capt – James Brown
West Bromwich Albion: Bob Roberts, Harry Green, Harry Bell, Ezra Horton, Charlie Perry, George Timmins, George Woodhall, Tom Green, capt – Jimmy Bayliss, Arthur Loach, George Bell

Longest unbeaten run in FA Cup history
Having won the cup three times in a row it is hardly surprising that Blackburn Rovers hold the record for the longest unbeaten run in the FA Cup, because after losing to Darwen on December 2nd 1882 it wasn't

to be until Scottish club Renton beat them in a first round replay on November 27th 1886 that they lost again. Blackburn were undefeated for 23 matches, including 20 consecutive victories.

1889–90 – Won
Round 1
Sunderland H 4-2 aet
Townley 2, Campbell, Barton
Round 2
Grimsby Town H 3-0
Arnold, Ogilvie (og), Jack Southworth
Round 3
Bootle A 7-0
Walton 3, Jack Southworth 2, Forbes, Townley
Semi-Final
Wolverhampton Wanderers 1-0
Jack Southworth
Played at Derby Racecourse Ground, March 8th 1890
Final
The Wednesday 6-1
Blackburn: Townley 6, Walton 20, Townley 35, Southworth 45, Townley 75, Lofthouse 80
Wednesday: Mumford 60
Played at Kennington Oval, March 29th 1890

Blackburn: Jack Horne, James Southworth, John Forbes, John Barton, George Dewar, Jimmy Forrest, Joe Lofthouse, Harry Campbell, Jack Southworth, Nat Walton, William Townley
The Wednesday: John Smith, Haydn Morley, Edward

Appendix Three

Brayshaw, Jack Dungworth, Billy Betts, George Waller, Billy Ingham, Harry Woodhouse, Michael Bennett, Albert Mumford, Tom Cawley

Twenty thousand were present to watch the most one-sided FA Cup final since the competition started. Although Blackburn were pre-match favourites, no one could have anticipated how unnerved their opponents would be.

It took Blackburn little more than five minutes to take the lead. It came after Dungworth handled and when Forrest passed to Townley his shot took a slight deflection on its way past Smith in the Wednesday goal.

By half-time it was 4-0 and although Sheffield showed great spirit at the start of the second half they were grateful for Smith in their goal for keeping the score down.

Mumford had the temerity to score for The Wednesday but Townley became the first man to score a cup final hat-trick and then Lofthouse made it 6-1. The crowd broke into the enclosure and rushed for the grandstand to try to ensure a decent vantage spot to witness the trophy presentation. By winning the FA Cup with Blackburn Harry Campbell became the first player to win the English and Scottish FA Cups, having won the latter with Renton in 1888.

1890–91 – Won
Round 1
Middlesbrough Ironopolis A 2-1 aet

Jack Southworth, Hall
FA ordered replay after protest
R Middlesbrough Ironopolis A 3-0
Hall 2, Stevenson (og)

Round 2
Chester H 7-0
Jack Southworth 3, Hall, Townley, Taylor (og), AN other
Round 3
Wolverhampton H 2-0
Baugh (og), Fletcher (og)
Semi-Final
WBA 3-2
Jack Southworth, Hall, AN Other
Played at Victoria Ground, Stoke, February 28th 1891
Final
Blackburn 3 Notts County 1
Blackburn: Dewar 8, Jack Southworth 30, Townley 35
Notts County: Oswald 70
Played at Kennington Oval, March 21st 1891

Blackburn: Rowland Pennington, Tom Brandon, capt – John Forbes, John Barton, George Dewar, Jimmy Forrest, Joe Lofthouse, Nat Walton, Jack Southworth, Combe Hall, William Townley
Notts County: James Thraves, Alex Ferguson, John Hendry, Archibald Osborne, David Calderhead, Alf Shelton, Andrew McGregor, Thomas McInnes, capt – Jack Oswald, William Locker, Harry Daft

Appendix Three

Blackburn won the FA Cup for a second consecutive year to make it a grand total of five wins, equal to the number of victories recorded by The Wanderers. Although Notts County had beaten their opponents 7-1 in a league match played at Blackburn the previous weekend no one was under any illusions that this would be a comfortable victory for the Nottingham side, who were playing in their first final.

And within eight minutes it became even more difficult when a Lofthouse throw-in was never properly cleared and Dewar forced home the loose ball to the cheers of the Rovers fans in the 23,000 crowd, who together paid £1,454 to watch the game. Southworth made it two on the half-hour mark and Townley scored his fourth FA Cup final goal by making it 3-0 with a header a few minutes later. Notts County did reduce the arrears through Oswald but with the goal coming with only 20 minutes remaining there was never any real prospect of an unlikely recovery.

1927–28 – Won
Round 3
Newcastle United H 4-1
Puddefoot, Mitchell 2, Thornewell
Round 4
Exeter City A 2-2
Roscamp, Rigby
R Exeter City H 3-1 aet
Roscamp, Mitchell, Puddefoot
Round 5

Port Vale H 2-1
Roscamp, Mitchell
Quarter-final
Manchester United H 2-0
Puddefoot 2
Semi-final
Arsenal 1-0
Roscamp
Played at Filbert Street, Leicester, March 24th 1928
Final
Blackburn 3 Huddersfield 1
Blackburn: Roscamp 1, 85, McLean 22
Huddersfield: Jackson, 55
Played at Wembley Empire Stadium, April 21st 1928

Blackburn: Jock Crawford, Jock Hutton, Herbert Jones, captain – Harry Healless, Willie Rankin, Austin Campbell, George Thornewell, Syd Puddefoot, Jack Roscamp, Tommy McLean, Arthur Rigby
Huddersfield: Billy Mercer, Roy Goodall, Ned Barkas, Levi Redfern, Tommy Wilson, David Steele, Alex Jackson, Bob Kelly, George Brown, capt – Clem Stephenson, Billy Smith

Having won their semi-final at the first attempt, Blackburn were forced to wait to find out who they would play after Yorkshire rivals Sheffield United and Huddersfield Town drew twice before a single goal from Alex Jackson was enough to see 'The Terriers' through to Wembley, where both finalists would be playing for the first time.

Appendix Three

Not surprisingly, in light of the fact that Huddersfield had completed a league treble between 1924 and 1926 and then had ended up as runners-up in the next two seasons, they were clear favourites to win the cup for the first time in their relatively short history.

Yet within less than sixty seconds Blackburn, looking to equal Villa's record of winning the trophy six times, were ahead. The goal came when Roscamp, chasing what appeared a wasted ball from Healless's cross, bundled both the Terriers' keeper Mercer and the ball into the net. Today it would bring a certain free kick and possibly a yellow card but not so in those days and there was no question of referee T.G. Bryan disallowing the goal.

Rovers scored a second on 22 minutes and it was a cracking goal when McLean finished off a fine move driving home from just inside the penalty area.

Huddersfield at last retaliated but the Rovers defence was in fine form and at half-time the score remained Blackburn Rovers 2 Huddersfield 0. The Yorkshire side did manage to get back into the game on 55 minutes when Jackson was the scorer despite a desperate dive by Crawford. Stephenson might then have equalised with a header.

Roscamp got his just rewards for a fine performance with Rovers' third.

The crowd was 92,041 which produced receipts of £23,238.

Fifty Years On

Wolverhampton Wanderers

1888–89 – Lost
Round 1 Old Carthusians H 4-3
Wood 2, Wykes, Mason
Round 2
Walsall Town Swifts H 6-1
Knight 3, Hunter, Lowder, Brodie
Quarter-final
Sheffield Wednesday H 3-0
Wykes 2 Fletcher
Semi-final
Blackburn Rovers 1-1
Wykes
Played at Alexandra Ground, Crewe, March 16th 1889
R Blackburn Rovers 3-1
Allen, Hunter, Wood
Played at Alexandra Ground, Crewe, March 23rd 1889
Final
Preston North End 0-3
PNE: Dewhurst 5, Ross 25, Thomson 70
Played at Kennington Oval, March 30th 1889
Preston North End: (Dr) Robert-Mills Roberts, Rob Howarth, Bob Holmes, George Drummond, David Russell, Johnny Graham, Jack Gordon, John Goodall, capt – Fred Dewhurst Sam Thompson, Jimmy Ross
Wolves: Jackie Baynton, Dickie Baugh, Charlie Mason, Albert Fletcher, Harry Allen, Arthur Lowder, Tommy Hunter, David Wykes, John Brodie (c), Harry Wood, Tom Knight

Appendix Three

In light of the fact that Preston North End had won the inaugural Division 1 title without losing a single game, the outcome of Wolves' first ever appearance in the FA Cup final was no major surprise. Preston's success meant they became the first club to complete the League and Cup 'double' in the same season, thus earning themselves the nickname of The Invincibles.

Wolves' failure to score meant Preston won the Cup without conceding a goal. Although Preston had stayed overnight in London, Wolves arrived in the capital at around dinnertime on the Saturday. The crowd was a record 22,000.

Preston took the lead after quarter of an hour. Fred Dewhurst, Preston's captain and scorer of their goal the previous year when they lost 2-1 to WBA, scored the first. Preston made it 2-0 after 25 minutes, when Baynton allowed a shot from Ross to slip under him. Jack Baynton's appearance in the final was one of only 28 for the club but without him the club may never have existed as he helped form them with his best friend, John Brodie, and later went on to captain the side when the club's first trophy, the Wrekin Cup in 1884, was captured.

Hunter, Knight and the Wolves captain Brodie, who had moved from Preston, gave hope to the Wolves followers with decent shots at goal. Brodie had only just made his England international debut, captaining his country and scoring on March 2nd that year as England beat Ireland 6-1 at Anfield.

Preston's third came on 70 minutes when

Thompson, following up, had the simple task of knocking home a rebound.

A single sheet programme from this final achieved a world record price of £21,850 at Graham Budd Auctions in London. The estimate had been around £10,000.

1892–93 – Winners

Round 1
Bolton Wanderers A 1-1 aet
Johnston
R Bolton Wanderers H 2-1
Wood, Wykes

Round 2
Middlesbrough H 2-1 aet
Wykes, Butcher

Quarter-final
Darwen H 5-0 Topham 2, Wykes, Butcher, Griffin

Semi-final
Blackburn Rovers 2-1
Topham Butcher
Played at Town Ground, Nottingham, March 4th 1893

Final
Everton 1-0
Allen 60
Played at Fallowfield, Manchester, March 25th 1893

Wolves: Billy Rose, Dick Baugh, George Swift, Billy Malpass, capt – Harry Allen, George Kinsey, Dick Topham, David Wykes, Joe Butcher, Alf Griffin, Harry Wood

Everton: Richard Williams, Bob Kelso, Bob Howarth,

Appendix Three

Richard Boyle, Johnny Holt, Alex Stewart, Alex Latta, Patrick Gordon, Alex Maxwell, Edgar Chadwick, Alf Millward

A record crowd officially recorded as 45,000* were present to witness Wolves winning the FA Cup for the first time. So many had wanted to go from Wolverhampton that employers had been under pressure to call a general holiday. In addition, with football becoming increasingly popular, the railway companies, scenting an opportunity to profit, had taken to running special trains from all parts of the country to the Cup Final.

Bookmakers had the Liverpool side as slight favourites although Wolves featured four of their unsuccessful cup final side of four years before in Baugh, Allen, Wykes and Wood. Everton, with a team packed with reserves, had beaten Wolves at Molineux 4-2 the previous weekend but this was to be Wolves' day.

The match began, however, with Everton pushing forward but they found the Wolves half-back line of Malpass, Allen and Kinsey in determined mood, the last-named's fine performance bringing in its wake selection for the England team which faced Scotland the following Saturday. The team also contained two from the defeated Everton side in Holt and Chadwick.

As Wolves' confidence grew, Everton were forced to rely on a last-ditch Kelso tackle to prevent a certain goal. The Merseysiders' left-winger Millward wasted by far the best first-half chance. He was to be unfortunate in FA Cup finals, playing in three, two with Everton and one with Southampton, and losing all three.

At half-time the score remained goalless and it stayed that way until 15 minutes into the second half, when Wolves scored the only goal. It was Allen, the Wolves captain, who brought tears of joy to the eyes of Black Countrymen when his dropping shot from range beat Williams.

The first man to raise the cup on behalf of Wolves, Harry Allen was a fine centre-half during a period in the game when much of a team's play was dictated from such a position. In addition to being a fine passer he was a strong tackler and good in the air. Allen unfortunately died at an early age, just 29, in 1895.

* It is estimated that more than 60,000 actually gained entry. With the sheer numbers causing a delay to the kick-off and ensuring that the pitch was often encroached upon during the match Everton demanded, without success, a replay, arguing that conditions for a competitive match had been absent.

1895–96 – Lost
Round 1
Notts County H 2-2
Henderson, Malpass
R Notts County A 4-3
Wood 2, Beats, Black
Round 2

Appendix Three

Liverpool H 2-0
Wood, Owen
Quarter-final
Stoke H 3-0
Tonks, Henderson, Malpass
Semi-final
Derby County 2-1
Tonks, Malpass
Played at Perry Barr, Birmingham, March 21st 1896
Final
The Wednesday 1-2
Wednesday: Spiksley 1, 15
Wolves: Black 8
Played at Crystal Palace, April 18th 1896

Wolves: Billy Tennant, capt – Dick Baugh, Tom Dunn, Billy Owen, Billy Malpass, Hill Griffiths, Joe Tonks, Charlie Henderson, Billy Beats, Harry Wood, David Black
The Wednesday: Joe Massey, capt – Jack Earp, Ambrose Langley, Harry Brandon, Tom Crawshaw, Bob Petrie, Archie Brash, Alex Brady, Laurie Bell, Harry Davis, Fred Spiksley

The Wolves side contained just two players from their triumph of three years before – captain Dick Baugh (senior) and Harry Wood. Baugh went on to make 229 first team Wolves appearances at full back. He played twice for England. Wood's two spells with Wolves were split by an unhappy four-month spell with neighbours Walsall in 1891. He was a fine player who rammed home 126 goals in 289 appearances from his inside forward position.

The match attracted a record crowd of 48,836, close to 4,000 more than the previous record of 45,000 at the 1893 final, to Crystal Palace. Any latecomers would have missed a sensational start when The Wednesday, seeking their first cup success, took the lead after just 20 seconds.

According to the match report in the *Manchester Guardian*: "Scarcely 20 seconds had passed before the Wednesday scored the first point. Brash on the outside right passed across and Spiksley on the outside left put in a shot which Tennant failed to reach." This would make Spiksley's goal the quickest ever goal in an FA Cup final.

Outside left Fred Spiksley was one of the Wednesday early greats, scoring more than a hundred goals in over 300 first team appearances. He also played seven times for England, scoring five times and helping his country to two Home Championships, in 1893 and 1896. When he retired in 1906 he became famous as a coach/manager, helping AIK Stockholm to the Swedish Championship. He also managed TSV 1860 München – he was interned when World War I broke out and found himself spending time playing football with other famous ex-pros in Steve Bloomer, Fred Pentland and Sam Wolstenholme – and Real Club Espana.

If Wolves were disappointed by falling behind so early they didn't show it and on eight minutes outside left David Black scored. On 18 minutes

Appendix Three

Spiksley scored a second.

In the second half there was a moment when Wolves followers believed their side had scored but an indirect free kick had passed directly between the posts without the ball having been touched by another player.

The Wednesday were being constantly pressed back but the shooting of the Wolves forwards was poor and the match ended with a 2-1 victory for the Sheffield side.

When the Wednesday captain Jack Earp went up to collect the trophy he was presented with the second FA Cup. This was because the first had been stolen from the window of a Birmingham shoe shop belonging to William Shilcock while held by Aston Villa on 11 September 1895. It was never seen again. But the new one was identical because after Wolves had won the Cup in 1893, the club's chairman had obtained permission from the Football Association to present each player with a ten-inch high silver replica of the trophy. One of these models was used as a model for the new cup.

1907–08 – Winners
Round 1
Bradford City A 1-1
Shelton
R Bradford City H 1-0
Hedley
Round 2
Bury H 2-0

Radford 2
Round 3
Swindon Town H 2-0
Harrison, Hedley
Quarter-final
Stoke A 1-0
Radford
Semi-final
Southampton 2-0
Radford, Hedley
Played at Stamford Bridge, March 28th 1908
Final
Newcastle United 3-1
Wolves: Hunt 40, Hedley 43, Harrison 85
Newcastle: Howie 73
Played at Crystal Palace Park, April 25th 1908

Wolves: Tommy Lunn, Jack Jones, Ted Collins, Kenneth Hunt, capt – Billy Wooldridge, Alf Bishop, Billy Harrison, Jack Shelton, George Hedley, Wally Radford, Jack Pedley
Newcastle: Jimmy Lawrence, Billy McCracken, Dick Pudan, Alex Gardner, capt – Colin Veitch, Peter McWilliam, Jock Rutherford, James Howie, Bill Appleyard, Finlay Speedie, George Wilson

The result was a major surprise, Newcastle United were the richest club in the land with a wealth of internationals even among their reserves, while Wolverhampton weren't even in the First Division. Newcastle had thrashed Fulham 6-0 in the semi-final,

Appendix Three

a record margin for that stage of the competition which still stands.

Wolves were all passion, drive and determination while Newcastle favoured a shorter passing game and for half an hour it was difficult to guess which would prove the most efficient. However, the pouring rain made the pitch increasingly heavy and it was the side from the West Midlands that began to assert control.

With only five minutes of the first half remaining it looked very much like both sides would run off without scoring. Three minutes later, however, it was 2-0 to Wolves. First, Reverend Kenneth Hunt received a pass after a brilliant run from Billy Harrison. As he cut in to hit his shot, Lawrence was well placed to save but the ball was wet and it slipped through his fingers and into the net. George Hedley scored the second from five yards. The goal made him the first player to score for two sides in the cup final as he had also scored for Sheffield United in 1902. Since then only Frank Stapleton and Ian Wright have achieved this feat.

Perhaps not surprisingly, Newcastle were on top in the second half. Attack was their only option but the Wolves defence were in fine form with Hunt, Wooldridge and Bishop forming a solid halfback line in front of full backs Jack Jones and Ted Collins. Howie reduced the arrears with seventeen minutes remaining but as Newcastle pressed in search of an equaliser Wolves, with five minutes left, scored their third and decisive goal.

It came from the best player on the pitch, right-winger Billy Harrison, who, taking matters into his own hands, beat the Newcastle half and full backs before advancing on Lawrence and finishing coolly.

Harrison had only joined Wolves at the start of the 1907–08 season but went on to have a long association with the club, making close to 350 first team appearances in which he scored 49 goals – although none as good as the one he scored in the final.

With the score at 3-1 there was no way back for Newcastle, who came off having played three cup finals in four years and lost every one.

1920–21 – Lost
Round 1
Stoke H 3-2
Edmonds 2 Burrill
Round 2
Derby County a 1-1
Wrightman og
R Derby County H 1-0
Richards
Round 3
Fulham A 1-0
Potts
Quarter-final
Everton A 1-0
Edmonds
Semi-final
Cardiff City 0-0

Appendix Three

Played at Anfield, March 19th 1921
Replay 3-1
Richards, Edmonds, Brooks
Played at Old Trafford, March 23rd 1921
Final
Tottenham Hotspur 0-1
Spurs: Dimmock 55
Played at Stamford Bridge, April 23rd 1921

Wolves: Noel George, Maurice Woodward, George Marshall, capt – Val Gregory, Joe Hodnett, Alf Riley, Tancy Lea, Frank Burrill, George Edmonds, Arthur Potts, Sammy Brooks
Spurs: Alex Hunter, Tommy Clay, Bob McDonald, Bert Smith, Charlie Walters, capt – Arthur Grimsdell, Jimmy Banks, Jimmy Seed, Jimmy Cantrell, Bert Bliss, Jimmy Dimmock

Although Wolves were regarded as outsiders by the bookmakers, the Second Division side were determined to make a match of it with captain Val Gregory saying before the kick-off: "We shall do our best to create an upset. I know the Spurs are expected to win but so too were Everton and Newcastle United on the previous two occasions when Wolves have won the cup. We hope to win, but in any event we will put up a big fight."

In the excellent *Wolverhampton Wanderers – The Complete Record*, the author Tony Matthews describes Gregory as "an exceptionally smart tackler, aggressive and perceptive, and a purveyor of passes that could split the tightest of defences... he had urged his players on with some gritty performances in the FA Cup."

The match was watched by a crowd of more than 72,000. Among them were the King, George V, the Duke of York and the touring Australian cricket team. Any hopes of a thriller were ruined by a cloudburst that reduced the pitch to a quagmire and the match rarely rose to any great heights as a consequence.

Dimmock, the only local lad in the Spurs team, scored the game's solitary goal ten minutes after half-time when he won the ball back from Woodward, steadied himself and drove it low and hard into the far corner of the net. It was a deserved reward for the day's best performer.

Only once did Wolves look like they might equalise when, just before the end, after a fine run Sammy Brooks had his close-range shot brilliantly blocked by the Tottenham centre-half Charlie Walters, who threw his body in the way to prevent a certain goal.

Gregory was proud of his team's efforts, saying afterwards that: "We have fought and we have lost, but we made them work hard for their win. We are very disappointed not to go back to Wolverhampton without the Cup, but frankly I admit that the better team won. We are entitled to say, I think, that we did not disgrace ourselves. We did all we could and we played hard to the finish. We could do no more."

The result meant that Tottenham Hotspur

Appendix Three

recorded their second FA Cup success and their first as a League club, having previously won the Cup in 1900–01 while in the Southern League.

1938–39 – Lost

Round 3
Bradford Park Avenue H 3-1
Westcott 2, McIntosh

Round 4
Leicester City H 5-1
Westcott 2, Maguire 2, Dorsett

Round 5
Liverpool H 4-1
Westcott, McIntosh, Burton, Dorsett

Quarter-final
Everton H 2-0
Westcott 2

Semi-final
Grimsby Town 5-0
Westcott 4, Galley
Played at Old Trafford, March 25th 1939

Final
Portsmouth 1-4
Wolves: Dorsett 54
Portsmouth: Barlow 29, Anderson 43, Parker 46, 71
Played at Wembley Stadium, April 28th 1939
Attendance: 43,038. Receipts: £4,552

Wolves: Alec Scott, Billy Morris, Jack Taylor, Tom Galley, capt – Stan Cullis, Joe Gardiner, Stan Burton, Alex McIntosh, Dennis Westcott, Dickie Dorsett, Teddy Maguire

Fifty Years On

Portsmouth: George Walker, Lew Morgan, Bill Rochford, capt – Jimmy Guthrie, Tommy Rowe, Guy Wharton, Fred Worrall, Jimmy McAlinden, Jock Anderson, Bert Barlow, Cliff Parker

With some bookmakers laying 5-1 against Portsmouth winning the final, the result was one of the biggest shocks in the competition's history. Second-placed Wolves had roared to the final, scoring 19 goals against just three. Mid-table Portsmouth, looking to make it third time lucky having lost in the 1929 and 1934 finals against Bolton and Manchester City respectively, had also qualified impressively, winning all five of their games and conceding only a single goal in the process.

After the game much was made of how the Pompey players had drawn confidence before it when they were asked to sign an autograph book which revealed the shaky signatures of the Wolves side with one or two names unrecognisable. Portsmouth's opening goal came, ironically, from a Wolves corner. Fred Worrall, the only man from the unsuccessful Pompey side of 1934 to make it into the 1939 starting XI, flicked the ball over the Wolves back line for Bert Barlow to flash a terrific shot past Alec Scott. Fourteen minutes later it was 2-0 when a Lew Morgan clearance was helped on by Cliff Parker and when Worrall turned it inside to John Anderson, the centre-forward finished the move off in style.

Just after the restart Parker scored a third for Portsmouth when almost from the kick-off Barlow advanced to shoot and when Scott allowed the ball through his outstretched hands Parker was on hand to knock home the loose ball as it trickled towards the goal line.

Wolves reduced the arrears eight minutes later when Dicky Dorsett scored after a determined run. But try as manager Major Frank Buckley's team did, Wolves could not find an opportunity to put pressure on Portsmouth by making it 3-2.

Portsmouth made it 4-1 when, with 20 minutes left, Parker scored his second goal of the match. With the Second World War starting within months the south coast side were to hang on to the FA Cup for a record length of time: it would be seven years until Derby won it in 1946.

1948–49 – Winners
Round 3
Chesterfield H 6-0
Hancocks, Pye 2, Mullen, Smyth 2
Round 4
Sheffield United A 3-0
Hancocks 2, Dunn
Round 5
Liverpool H 3-1
Dunn, Smyth, Mullen
Quarter-final
WBA H 1-0
Mullen
Semi-final
Manchester United 1-1 aet

Fifty Years On

Smyth
Played at Hillsborough, 26.03.1949
R Manchester United 1-0
Smyth
Played at Goodison Park, April 2nd 1949
Final
Leicester City 3-1
Wolves: Pye 13, 42, Smyth 47
Leicester: Griffiths 46
Played at Wembley Stadium, April 30th 1949

Wolves: Bert Williams, Roy Pritchard, Terry Springthorpe, Billy Crook, Bill Shorthouse, Billy Wright (captain), Johnny Hancocks, Sammy Smyth, Jesse Pye, Jimmy Dunn, Jimmy Mullen
Leicester: Gordon Bradley, Horace Jelly, Alec Scott, Walter Harrison, Norman Plummer (captain), John King, Mal Griffiths, Jack Lee, Jim Harrison, Ken Chisholm, Charlie Adam

Just as in 1939, Wolves started the match as firm favourites. Leicester were struggling close to the bottom of Division 2 and knew they needed to win at least one of their remaining three league games after the final to stay in the division. The Foxes had also suffered the disappointment of losing one of their best players, Don Revie, who'd burst a blood vessel in his nose just three days before Wembley.

In comparison, Wolves were in sparkling form with only one defeat in 13 league and cup games. They had knocked out the cup holders Manchester

Appendix Three

United after a replayed semi-final, Stan Cullis's men hanging on to a tenacious draw in the first match after injuries to both full backs virtually reduced the side to nine men. One of the replay replacements, Terry Springthorpe, subsequently earned a place in the side at Wembley and later played for the USA.

From the start Wolves were in charge and it was no surprise when Johnny Hancocks, seizing on a slight hesitation by Alec Scott, crossed and Jesse Pye headed home. Pye had missed the five games before the final and, in his absence, a young Dennis Wilshaw had shown his skills by scoring seven times. Despite this Cullis had chosen to go with experience and his growing managerial reputation in 1949 increased when Pye scored a second just before half-time, nipping in just inches in front of Sammy Smyth to leave Bradley with no chance.

With Wolves 2-0 up there seemed to be no chance for the struggling Division 2 side. Yet Leicester had not reached the Cup final without showing some tenacity, beating First Division Birmingham City after three games in the third round, and overcoming Luton Town 5-3 in a fifth-round replay after the first match finished 5-5. In the semi-final they disposed of Portsmouth, who were to finish the season as Division One champions.

Within a minute of the restart Leicester had halved the arrears with a wonderful goal. A 40-yard run by left-winger Charlie Adam ended with Chisholm hitting a shot that Williams could only parry, which left Griffiths to prod the ball home. It was now a proper match, and it looked like Leicester had made it 2-2, but Chisholm was offside by the narrowest of margins.

It became a whole lot worse for Leicester when within 60 seconds Wolves had restored their two-goal advantage with a marvellous goal. Smyth beat three players before advancing to near the penalty spot and hitting a left-foot shot that whistled past Bradley. Smyth, a modest man, later admitted he had no idea why he'd struck the ball with his left foot as he was almost entirely reliant on his right. It didn't matter. Wolves had won the FA Cup for the third time and Billy Wright was a proud man when he became the first Wolves captain to collect the FA Cup at Wembley. It had been 41 years since the club had last won the trophy and, not surprisingly, when the team returned to the town they were welcomed by a massive cheering crowd of more than 70,000. Stan Cullis was building a fine side, one that would go on to greater glories as the 1950s unfolded.

Postscript

This is our day, the British Day, but it is a day that attracts the world, and so far as we are concerned, invest the national winter sport with something that not even the big money of the European Cup can really match.

Here we are on our own, but there is probably not a soccer occasion in the world to compare to the final of the Football Association Cup, the father of them all.

'Commentator' of the *Express and Star*

Other books from SportsBooks

William Garbutt – The Father of Italian Football
Paul Edgerton
In Italy managers are called "mister" and the habit goes back to William Garbutt, who, unable to play any more following injury at the age of 29, went from Blackburn Rovers to coach Genoa. He also coached Roma, Napoli, AC Milan and Athletic Bilbao during a career which also saw him help coach the Italian national team.
9781899807826
£7.99
Paperbak

A Develyshe Pastime
Graham Hughes
The modern game of football is thought to have its origins in 12th century England. Certainly once the Victorians began organising it in the latter half of the 19th century it spread around the world in various forms. American and Canadian football, Rugby League and Union, Aussies Rules and Gaelic football all have their roots in the rough games played between villages in mediaeval England. Graham Hughes traces the paths the various disciplines took and profiles the men who turned them into major sports.
9781899807796
£17.99
Hardback

Chapped Legs and Punctured Balls
Paul Cooper lived for football like most other 1960s kids and this is his account, both hilarious and nostalgic, of the things that went with the game in those more innocent times – the clothes and shoes kids wore, the balls they played with, from the very rare leather case ball with its occasionally crippling lace to the stone that was used in the playground if nothing else was available.

9781899807772
£5.99
Paperback

Passport to Football
Stuart Fuller, author of four books of travel guides to football and a well-known blogger on football related matters, brings together his experiences on watching football in far-flung places too numerous to mention here, although they do include Moscow, Macedonia, Klagenfurt, Budapest, and Kazakhstan.
Stuart brings an experienced and humorous eye to the business of watching the beautiful game, noting for example that in a game between Istanbul BBS and Rizaspor an off-side goal was allowed to stand because the linesman was arguing with the bench of the team against which he had just given a free-kick!
9781899807833
£14.99
Paperback

Tales from the Gwladys Street
Fans have been having a rough time of it in recent years. Clubs have hiked their admission prices while TV demands have resulted in odd kick-off times which often mean difficult journeys. But still they flock to football matches. This book tells the story of one club, Everton, through the mouths of their fans and players. The resulting stories show how obsessive football fans can be and how they seek humour in every situation. The stories are from Evertonians but the type of experiences recalled are not unique to one club.
9781899807895
£12.99
Paperback

Finn McCool's Football Club
Stephen Rea was a typical ex-pat in the US. The former Belfast journalist needed somewhere to watch and play football (or soccer as they insist on calling it over there). He found Finn McCool's Irish bar where a diverse collection of nationalities

made up the regulars and the football team. They even began to get serious, joining a league. But then Hurricane Katrina struck. Rea's book is both a wry look at an obsession with football and an account of what happened to some of those who suffered one of the US's worst disasters, with an official death toll of 1,100. Many of the team and pub regulars were among those affected by the tragedy.
9781899807864
£8.99
Paperback

Modern Football is Rubbish
Nick Davidson and Shaun Hunt are going through a midlife crisis as far as football is concerned. Now they've reached early middle-age they are wondering what has happened to the beautiful game. Where have all the muddy pitches gone they wonder? They wallow in nostalgia for 3pm Saturday kick-offs and cup upsets and they rant against inflated egos, spiralling salaries and satellite TV. And they wonder about men in tights and gloves.
9781899807710
£6.88
Paperback

Charlie Hurley – "The Greatest Centre Half the World has ever seen"
Mark Metcalf
Charlie Hurley was not only a great player, he was one of the characters who illuminated football in the 1950s and '60s. His story will attract great coverage in the papers as he tells of clashes with another footballing great, Jim Baxter, his disputes with the board at Reading when he became a manager and the uncompromising attitude of players and managers during his playing days. Born in Cork, but raised in Essex from the age of seven months, Charlie started his playing career with Millwall before joining Sunderland in 1957. He was to make 400 appearances before leaving for Bolton Wanderers in 1969.
9781899807 69 7
Price £17.99
Hardback

The World at their Feet – Northern Ireland in Sweden
Ronnie Hanna
The story of Northern Ireland's first trip to the World Cup finals, when, despite being the smallest country, they reached the quarter-finals.
9781899807 74 1
Price £7.99
Paperback

Memories of George Best
Chris Hilton & Ian Cole
Malcolm Brodie, of the *Belfast Telegraph* who covered George Best throughout his brilliant and ill-starred career, called this "the best Best book ever". The authors talked to many of the Manchester United star's contemporaries to find out the true story of the wayward genius.
9781899807 57 4
Price £14.99
Paperback

From Sheffield with Love
Brendan Murphy
Published to celebrate the 150th anniversary of Sheffield FC, the world's oldest football club. The book charts the rise of organised football in Sheffield and Nottingham, the two oldest centres of the game.
9781899807 56 7
Price £8.99
Paperback

The Irish Uprising
Andy Dawson
The story of Roy Keane's dramatic first season at Sunderland, which ended with promotion to the Premier League.
9781899807 60 4
Price £10.99
Paperback

Accrington Stanley – the club that wouldn't die
Phil Whalley

Fan and writer Phil Whalley charts the comeback of Accrington Stanley the club which resigned from the Football League in the early '60s. After going bust they re-formed in 1968 and began an astonishing climb back to the League.
1899807 47 0
Price £16.99
Hardback

The Rebel Tours – Cricket's Crisis of Conscience
Peter May
The title says it all. After the d'Oliveira affair cut official ties between South Africa and England, the leading players organised tours of the Republic under the slogan that sport and politics should not mix. The reaction of the English establishment shows in the cover. Mike Gatting, David Graveney and John Emburey face the press and although they were all banned from the international game all three were welcomed back into the establishment with a rapidity that disturbed some obserrvers. Peter May talked to the people involved on both sides of the fence.
9781899807802
£17.99
Hardback